EZEKIEL

J. Vernon McGee

THOMAS NELSON PUBLISHERS

Nashville • Atlanta • London • Vancouver

Published in Nashville, Tennessee, by Thomas Nelson, Inc.

Scripture quotations are from the KING JAMES VERSION of the Bible.

Library of Congress Cataloging-in-Publication Data

McGee, J. Vernon (John Vernon), 1904–1988
   [Thru the Bible with J. Vernon McGee]
   Thru the Bible commentary series / J. Vernon McGee.
     p.   cm.
   Reprint. Originally published: Thru the Bible with J. Vernon McGee. 1975.
   Includes bibliographical references.
   ISBN 0-7852-1026-1 (TR)
   ISBN 0-7852-1086-5 (NRM)
   1. Bible—Commentaries. I. Title.
BS491.2.M37 1991
220.7′7—dc20   90–41340
                              CIP

Printed in the United States of America

8 9 — 99

CONTENTS

Preface v

Introduction vii

Outline x

Chapter 1 13

Chapters 2 and 3 22

Chapters 4 and 5 34

Chapter 6 39

Chapter 7 46

Chapter 8 54

Chapters 9 and 10 61

Chapters 11—13 70

Chapters 14—16 81

Chapter 17 92

Chapters 18 and 19 95

Chapter 20 102

Chapter 21 107

Chapters 22—24 114

Chapter 25 123

Chapter 26 128

Chapter 27 133

Chapter 28 136

Chapters 29 and 30 144

Chapters 31 and 32 151

Chapter 33 160

Chapter 34 169

Chapters 35 and 36 176
Chapter 37 182
Chapters 38 and 39 190
Chapters 40—48 206
Bibliography 216

PREFACE

The radio broadcasts of the Thru the Bible Radio five-year program were transcribed, edited, and published first in single-volume paperbacks to accommodate the radio audience.

There has been a minimal amount of further editing for this publication. Therefore, these messages are not the word-for-word recording of the taped messages which went out over the air. The changes were necessary to accommodate a reading audience rather than a listening audience.

These are popular messages, prepared originally for a radio audience. They should not be considered a commentary on the entire Bible in any sense of that term. These messages are devoid of any attempt to present a theological or technical commentary on the Bible. Behind these messages is a great deal of research and study in order to interpret the Bible from a popular rather than from a scholarly (and too-often boring) viewpoint.

We have definitely and deliberately attempted "to put the cookies on the bottom shelf so that the kiddies could get them."

The fact that these messages have been translated into many languages for radio broadcasting and have been received with enthusiasm reveals the need for a simple teaching of the whole Bible for the masses of the world.

I am indebted to many people and to many sources for bringing this volume into existence. I should express my especial thanks to my secretary, Gertrude Cutler, who supervised the editorial work; to Dr. Elliott R. Cole, my associate, who handled all the detailed work with the publishers; and finally, to my wife Ruth for tenaciously encouraging me from the beginning to put my notes and messages into printed form.

Solomon wrote, ". . . of making many books there is no end; and much study is a weariness of the flesh" (Eccl. 12:12). On a sea of books that flood the marketplace, we launch this series of THRU THE BIBLE with the hope that it might draw many to the one Book, *The Bible.*

J. VERNON McGEE

The Book of
EZEKIEL

INTRODUCTION

Ezekiel was a priest (Ezek. 1:3), but he never served in that office because he was taken captive to Babylon during the reign of Jehoiachin (2 Kings 24:10–16), who was the king of Judah who followed Jehoiakim. It was during the eleven-year reign of Jehoiakim that the first deportation took place when Daniel was taken captive. Jehoiachin then came to the throne and reigned only three months. In 597 B.C. the second deportation took place, and Ezekiel was taken captive.

Ezekiel was a contemporary of Jeremiah and Daniel. Jeremiah was an old man at this time. He had begun his ministry as a young man during the reign of young King Josiah. He had remained with the remnant in the land and then was taken by them down into Egypt. Therefore his ministry at this time was confined to the remnant in Egypt. Daniel had been taken into the court of the king of Babylon and had become his prime minister. Ezekiel, then, was with the captives who had been brought down to the rivers of Babylon. The captives had been placed by the great canal that came off the River Euphrates, which was several miles from Babylon itself. Ezekiel's ministry was among those people.

Psalm 137 is the psalm of the remnant in Babylon: "By the rivers of Babylon, there we sat down, yea, we wept, when we remembered Zion. We hanged our harps upon the willows in the midst thereof" (Ps. 137:1–2). But at the same time Ezekiel writes: "The heavens were opened, and I saw visions of God" (Ezek. 1:1). What a contrast! While these people had already put their harps on a willow tree and sat down to weep, this man Ezekiel was seeing visions of God!

Jeremiah, Ezekiel, and Daniel were all prophets, but each had a particular and peculiar ministry to a certain group of people, and apparently they never came into contact with each other. From the record in the Book of Daniel you would not gather that Daniel ever visited his people in Babylon where Ezekiel was; yet he had a great concern for them and he actually defended them. But did Daniel and Jeremiah know each other? Well, we know from his book that Daniel was acquainted with the prophecies of Jeremiah. I have a notion that as a young man in his teens he listened to Jeremiah in Jerusalem. Ezekiel also was a young man when he was taken captive, and he too had probably heard Jeremiah, but had no personal acquaintance with Daniel.

The message of Ezekiel is the most spiritual of all the prophets because he dealt particularly with the Person of God. Someone has said, "Ezekiel is the prophet of the Spirit, as Isaiah is the prophet of the Son, and Jeremiah the prophet of the Father."

During the first years of the captivity the false prophets were still saying that the people were going to return to Jerusalem and that the city would not be destroyed. The city was not destroyed even at the time of the second deportation. It was not until about 586 B.C., when Nebuchadnezzar came against the city the third time, that he burned and destroyed Jerusalem. Therefore for a period of about ten years, these false prophets were saying that the people would return and the city would not be destroyed. Jeremiah had sent a message to Babylon saying the city would be destroyed, and Ezekiel confirmed his message. He warned the people that they must turn to God before they could return to Jerusalem. When the time came, a very small remnant did turn to God, and they returned to Jerusalem very discouraged.

Ezekiel began his ministry five years after he was taken captive at about the age of thirty. In many ways, he spoke in the darkest days of the nation. He stood at the bottom of a valley in the darkest corner. He had to meet the false hope given by the false prophets and the indifference and despondency begotten in the days of sin and disaster. The people would not listen to his message. Therefore, he resorted to a new method. Instead of speaking in parables, as the Lord Jesus did, he acted out the parables. He actually did some very interesting stunts.

We read in Ezekiel 24:24, "Thus Ezekiel is unto you a sign: according to all that he hath done shall ye do: and when this cometh, ye shall know that I am the Lord GOD." The people would not listen to his words, so he would act them out, and he attracted a great deal of attention that way.

We have folk who use this very same method today. We have placard carriers, flagpole sitters, and walkathons. People do these things to attract attention and gain publicity. This, too, was Ezekiel's method. One time he walked into a house, locked himself in, and then started digging himself out. When he came out, he came out in the middle of the street! Here in Pasadena, California, it is nothing new to be digging in the middle of the street, for the city workers keep digging up the streets all the time. But in Ezekiel's time, when a man came up out of the middle of the street one day, people naturally gathered around and said, "What's the big idea?" Ezekiel had a message for them, and he gave it to them (see Ezek. 12:8–16).

Ezekiel is the prophet of the glory of the Lord. There were three prophets of Israel who spoke when they were out of the land. They are Ezekiel, Daniel, and John (who wrote from the island of Patmos). All three of these men wrote what is called an apocalypse. They all used highly symbolic language; yet they saw the brightest light and held the highest hope of all the prophets. Ezekiel saw the Shekinah glory of the Lord leave Solomon's temple, but he also saw the return of the glory of the Lord which was projected into the future and will come to pass during the Kingdom Age, or the Millennium.

The meaning of Ezekiel is seen in this coming of the glory during the Kingdom Age. Ezekiel looked beyond the sufferings of Christ to the glory that should follow. As Peter said of the prophets, they saw the sufferings and they saw the glory that would follow (1 Pet. 1:11). I think Ezekiel saw it better than any of the other prophets.

OUTLINE

I. **Glory of the Lord; Commission of the Prophets, Chapters 1—7**
   A. Display of the Glory, Chapter 1
   B. Prophet's Call and Endowment with Power for the Office, Chapter 2
   C. Prophet's Preparation; Office as Watchman, Chapter 3
   D. Judgment of Jerusalem, Chapter 4
   E. Sign of Prophet Shaving Hair, Chapter 5
   F. Sword to Fall Upon Jerusalem; Remnant to be Saved, Chapter 6
   G. Prophecy of Final Destruction of Jerusalem, Chapter 7

II. **Glory of the Lord; Compete Captivity of Jerusalem and Israel; Departure of the Glory, Chapters 8—24**
   A. Vision of the Glory; Temple Defilement by Idolatry Explains its Destruction, Chapter 8
   B. Shekinah Glory Prepares to Leave Temple, Chapter 9
   C. Shekinah Glory Fills Holy Place; Leaves the Temple, Chapter 10
   D. Prophecy Against Rulers of Jerusalem, Chapter 11
   E. Ezekiel Enacts Destruction of Jerusalem, Chapter 12
   F. Prophecy Against Pseudo Prophets and Prophetesses, Chapter 13
   G. Prophecy Against Idolatry of Elders; Certain Destruction of Jerusalem, Chapter 14
   H. Vision of the Vine, Chapter 15
   I. Jerusalem Likened to Abandoned Baby Adopted by God, Chapter 16
   J. Riddle of Two Eagles, Chapter 17
   K. Wages of Sin is Death, Chapter 18
   L. Elegy of Jehovah over Princes of Israel, Chapter 19
   M. Review of Sins of Nation; Future Judgment and Restoration, Chapter 20

N. King of Babylon to Remove Last King of Davidic Line Until Messiah Comes, Chapter 21
O. Review of Abominations of Jerusalem, Chapter 22
P. Parable of Two Sisters (Samaria and Jerusalem), Chapter 23
Q. Parable of Boiling Pot, Chapter 24

III. Glory of the Lord; Judgment of Nations, Chapters 25—32
A. Against Ammon, Moab, Edom, and Philistia, Chapter 25
B. Against Tyre, Chapters 26—28
C. Against Egypt, Chapters 29—32

IV. Glory of the Lord and the Coming Kingdom, Chapters 33—48
A. Recommission of the Prophet, Chapters 33—34
B. Restoration of Israel, Chapters 35—36
C. Resurrection of Israel, Chapter 37
D. Repudiation of Gog and Magog, Chapters 38—39
E. Rebuilt Temple, Chapters 40—42
F. Return of the Glory of the Lord, Chapters 43—48

CHAPTER 1

THEME: Display of the Lord's glory

Ezekiel's vision of the glory of the Lord may very well be a key to all of the visions in the entire Word of God; it certainly is the key to the rest of the Book of Ezekiel. Many people think of the Book of the Revelation as resting upon the prophecy of Daniel and the Olivet Discourse of our Lord. That is true, but I believe it rests primarily upon the apocalypse of Ezekiel; you will find a striking similarity between the vision in Ezekiel 1 and chapters 4 and 5 of Revelation.

This vision is a very difficult one to deal with. John Calvin said, "If anyone asks whether the vision is lucid, I confess its obscurity, and that I can scarcely understand it." I am certainly a Calvinist in the sense that I must concur with his statement—neither do I understand Ezekiel's vision clearly.

However, there is one thing that I am confident this vision is not: it is *not* a vision of the present mechanical age. Ezekiel's vision of the wheels within wheels is not a prophecy of the airplane! When the old propeller planes were first developed, several prophetic teachers were saying that this vision was a prophecy of the airplane. Today we have jet planes and they have no wheels within wheels, and we must set aside that interpretation. Such interpretations are juvenile. Silly and senile chatter like that is what has brought prophecy into disrepute.

What we do have in this first chapter of Ezekiel, I believe, is a vision of the glory of the Lord. In the Book of Isaiah we have the *principles* of the throne of God; in Jeremiah we have the *practice* of that throne; but in Ezekiel we have the *Person* who is on the throne. I want to hasten to add that we do not have God Himself exposed in this vision—you do not have a window display of Him. When I began my ministry I considered this to be a vision of God, but it is not that. It is instead a vision of the *glory* of God, a vision of the *presence* of God.

We see here a vision of the chariot of God as He rides triumphantly and irresistibly through time. There is one feature of this vision which shocked me when I discovered it: the chariot is vacant. I had taken for granted that God was there. There are four living creatures, the cherubim, connected with the chariot; yet they are distinct from it. Above all, there is a throne, and on the throne there is a Man. This is the highest vision of God that we are given, and it is most difficult to understand. We will note just a few of its impressive aspects:

Now it came to pass in the thirtieth year, in the fourth month, in the fifth day of the month, as I was among the captives by the river of Chebar, that the heavens were opened, and I saw visions of God [Ezek. 1:1].

"Now it came to pass in the thirtieth year" would seem to indicate that Ezekiel was thirty years of age. However, it is the belief of many scholars that this is geared to a little different calendar. I will not go into any detail on this as, frankly, it gets a little intricate, and I do not feel that it is essential.

"I saw visions of God." While the captives in Babylon had sat down and wept by the rivers of Babylon (see Ps. 137:1), Ezekiel was seeing visions of God. What a contrast—seeing visions and weeping!

In the fifth day of the month, which was the fifth year of king Jehoiachin's captivity [Ezek. 1:2].

We have not quite come to the time of the destruction of Jerusalem which took place during the reign of Zedekiah.

The word of the Lord came expressly unto Ezekiel the priest, the son of Buzi, in the land of the Chaldeans by the river Chebar; and the hand of the Lord was there upon him [Ezek. 1:3].

"The word of the Lord came expressly unto Ezekiel the priest." Ezekiel belonged to the tribe of Levi, apparently the priestly branch, and probably to the sons of Kohath. We are told that he was "the son of Buzi."

"Chebar" was the main canal that came off the Euphrates River, which watered that area. Evidently, the Jewish captives were put there to till the land. This area was removed by quite a few miles from Babylon, and that may be the reason that Daniel and Ezekiel did not have the opportunity to meet together for a meal. Daniel may have visited the area, but I doubt that Ezekiel would have been permitted to visit Daniel.

> **And I looked, and behold, a whirlwind came out of the north, a great cloud, and a fire infolding itself, and a brightness was about it, and out of the midst thereof as the colour of amber, out of the midst of the fire [Ezek. 1:4].**

"Behold, a whirlwind came out of the north." I know that many people have made a great deal of this idea that there is a great vacant space up yonder in the north and that this is the direction that leads to the presence of God. Our modern radio electronic telescopes with their big dishes have shown that there are stars out there—it is not vacant. However, "the north" is used in Scripture to point to the throne of God. In Isaiah 14:13 we read (speaking of the fall of Satan): "For thou hast said in thine heart, I will ascend into heaven, I will exalt my throne above the stars of God: I will sit also upon the mount of the congregation, in the sides of the north." I believe the idea is that, instead of pointing to the north pole, we are to look up—God's throne is out yonder, not relative to any direction at all. After all, its location is not something you and I can understand. We are told, ". . . look up . . . for your redemption draweth nigh" (Luke 21:28). That is the direction in which our attention should be focused today.

Also in Psalm 75:5–7 we read: "Lift not up your horn on high: speak not with a stiff neck. For promotion cometh neither from the east, nor from the west, nor from the south. But God is the judge: he putteth down one, and setteth up another." The only direction that is not mentioned is *north*, and I would say the thought is that it is *up*— God's throne is out yonder, even beyond space.

This whirlwind out of the north, then, indicates a tremendous movement from the throne of God—it is a judgment from God.

"And a fire infolding itself, and a brightness was about it, and out of the midst thereof as the colour of amber, out of the midst of the fire." This is the first thing we observe—a light flashing forth, revealing and also concealing. Obscuring and yet bringing out where it can be seen, it is a light brighter than the sun. Perhaps it could be compared to the inside of an atomic blast. It was incandescent, like lightning.

The Word of God says that ". . . our God is a consuming fire" (Heb. 12:29), and that ". . . God is light . . ." (1 John 1:5). Paul said that at the time of his conversion he saw ". . . a light from heaven, above the brightness of the sun . . ." (Acts 26:13). All of this speaks of the unapproachable presence of God (see also vv. 13–14).

> **Also out of the midst thereof came the likeness of four living creatures. And this was their appearance; they had the likeness of a man [Ezek. 1:5].**

This verse and also verse 26 ("the appearance of a man") speak of the incarnation of Christ, the fact that God became a man. "And the Word was made flesh, and dwelt [pitched His tent] among us . . ." (John 1:14). Isaiah 52:7 tells us, "How beautiful upon the mountains are the feet of him that bringeth good tidings, that publisheth peace; that bringeth good tidings of good, that publisheth salvation; that saith unto Zion, Thy God reigneth!" God came to earth a Man, walked the dusty trails of Palestine, and finally spikes were driven into His feet.

> **As for the likeness of their faces, they four had the face of man, and the face of a lion, on the right side: and they four had the face of an ox on the left side; they four also had the face of an eagle [Ezek. 1:10].**

These four faces (compare this with Rev. 4:6–8) remind us of the four Gospels in which Christ is revealed in four aspects: His kingship (Mathew) symbolized here by the lion; His servanthood (Mark) symbolized by the ox; His perfect humanity (Luke) symbolized by the face of a man; and His deity (John) symbolized by the flying eagle.

These four living creatures resemble the description we have of the cherubim who were in the Garden of Eden to guard the way of the Tree of Life. They were not shutting man out from God; they were keeping the way open. What did Adam and Eve see when they looked back as they left the garden? They saw a slain animal whose skins they were wearing. And they saw the cherubim overshadowing, keeping open the way to God. It is the blood that makes an atonement for the sin of man. When Moses made the mercy seat, there were cherubim above which looked down upon the blood of the sacrifices—the same thing Adam and Eve had seen. Through the blood is the only way man can approach God. The Lord Jesus said, ". . . no man cometh unto the Father, but by me" (John 14:6).

> **And they went every one straight forward: whither the spirit was to go, they went; and they turned not when they went [Ezek. 1:12].**

God is moving forward undeviatingly, unhesitatingly toward the accomplishment of His purpose in this world today. Nothing will deter Him—nothing can sidetrack Him at all.

> **As for the likeness of the living creatures, their appearance was like burning coals of fire, and like the appearance of lamps: it went up and down among the living creatures; and the fire was bright, and out of the fire went forth lightning.**
>
> **And the living creatures ran and returned as the appearance of a flash of lightning [Ezek. 1:13–14].**

The Scripture tells us ". . . God is light . . ." (1 John 1:5). This is a tremendous vision of the glory of God, a vision out of the person of God. The Lord Jesus said, ". . . I am the light of the world . . ." (John 8:12). What does this reveal to us? It reveals the righteousness and holiness of God. "But if we walk in the light, as he is in the light, we have fellowship one with another, and the blood of Jesus Christ his Son cleanseth us from all sin" (1 John 1:7). We would be scorched by the holiness of God if we had not been redeemed by the blood of Christ and covered with His righteousness.

God is not exposed in this vision—He is portrayed. It is still true that no man has seen God at any time. Moses said, ". . . Shew me thy glory," and God hid him in the cleft of the rock so that Moses saw only the glory of God, not the person of God. The Lord told him, ". . . Thou canst not see my face: for there shall no man see me, and live" (Exod. 33:18–23). Man has been forbidden to make a likeness of God (see Exod. 20:4). We do not know what He looks like. We do not even know how the Lord Jesus who became a man looked. But there is in the human heart a longing to see God; I think every idol witnesses to that desire. Although idols are perverted and profane representations, they reveal that men want to see God. Yet God has not chosen to reveal His Person to man.

> **Now as I beheld the living creatures, behold one wheel upon the earth by the living creatures, with his four faces.**
>
> **The appearance of the wheels and their work was like unto the colour of a beryl: and they four had one likeness: and their appearance and their work was as it were a wheel in the middle of a wheel [Ezek. 1:15–16].**

Again may I emphasize that this is not a prophecy of the present mechanical age or even of the invention of the wheel. I am sure that in the beginning man felled a tree, cut off part of the trunk, and found that he had a wheelbarrow. When he put two wheels on it, he had a cart. Then when he put four wheels on it, he had a Ford automobile! If that is what you want to see in this vision, may I say to you, that is silly and senile, that is garbage and rubbish. We need to read further to gain an understanding of these wheels within wheels.

> **As for their rings, they were so high that they were dreadful; and their rings were full of eyes round about them four [Ezek. 1:18].**

God is a God of intelligent purpose. You and I are not living in a universe that is moving into the future aimlessly and without purpose. God has a purpose for every atom which He has created, and He has a purpose for you, my friend, in His plan and program. The very fact that you and I are alive today reveals that we are to accomplish a purpose for God. God is intelligently carrying out His purpose in the world.

> **And when the living creatures went, the wheels went by them: and when the living creatures were lifted up from the earth, the wheels were lifted up.**
>
> **Whithersoever the spirit was to go, they went, thither was their spirit to go; and the wheels were lifted up over against them: for the spirit of the living creature was in the wheels [Ezek. 1:19–20].**

Now we can see more clearly that these wheels speak of the ceaseless activity and energy of God. Our God is omnipotent. The Lord Jesus said, ". . . All power is given unto me in heaven and in earth" (Matt. 28:18). God is moving forward, and He *will* accomplish His purposes.

In Revelation 4 we again read of these four living creatures of Ezekiel's vision. They are set to guard the throne of God, and in guarding the throne they do two things: (1) they protect the throne in the sense that they do not allow man in his sin to come into the presence of God; and (2) they indicate the way that man is to come. "I must needs go home by the way of the cross, there's no other way but this" ("The Way of the Cross Leads Home" by Jessie Brown Pounds). The cherubim show the way.

However, I think that Ezekiel saw something infinitely greater. He saw the cherubim over the world, extending mercy to this little piece of dirt that is flying through space. Someone has said that man "is nothing in the world but a rash on the epidermis of a second-rate planet." But God made the whole world a mercy seat when Christ died down here, and God is hovering over this world today, ready to receive any sinner who will come through Christ to Him.

> And above the firmament that was over their heads was
> the likeness of a throne, as the appearance of a sapphire
> stone: and upon the likeness of the throne was the like-
> ness as the appearance of a man above upon it.

> And I saw as the colour of amber, as the appearance of
> fire round about within it, from the appearance of his
> loins even upward, and from the appearance of his loins
> even downward, I saw as it were the appearance of fire,
> and it had brightness round about [Ezek. 1:26–27].

I see here an amber throne in the azure blue—a sapphire-studded throne flashing like a diamond and colored like a rainbow. The light blinds and obscures. The throne is filled with energy, like a missile on launching. It is moving like a chariot. It is not leaving the earth; it is coming to the earth. I see the cherubim over the world. I see a cross, a Lamb, and the blood. I see a mercy seat: there is mercy with the Lord. In the hymn "Only Trust Him" by J. H. Stockton we sing:

> Come, ev'ry soul by sin oppressed,
> There's mercy with the Lord.

In Romans 9:15 Paul wrote, "For he saith to Moses, I will have mercy on whom I will have mercy, and I will have compassion on whom I will have compassion." We are also told, "The soul that sinneth, it shall die" (Ezek. 18:20). God is saying to us—not only to the house of Israel, but to the whole world—"You *can* come to Me."

> As the appearance of the bow that is in the cloud in the
> day of rain, so was the appearance of the brightness
> round about. This was the appearance of the likeness of
> the glory of the LORD. And when I saw it, I fell upon my
> face, and I heard a voice of one that spake [Ezek. 1:28].

"This was the appearance of the likeness of the glory of the LORD." Ezekiel saw more than Moses saw, more than David, Isaiah, or Daniel saw. He saw a vision of the glory of God—not His Person, but His glory. The presence of God was there. When the Lord Jesus came to this earth and took upon Himself our humanity, His glory was not seen. Ezekiel saw the glory of the Lord.

"And when I saw it, I fell upon my face." This vision had a tremendous effect upon Ezekiel, and it should have this effect upon us: "Oh, God, I am undone. I'm lost and I need You. I turn to You and accept You."

We find throughout the Old Testament that when men came into the presence of God, they went down on their faces. This was true of Isaiah who said: ". . . Woe is me! for I am undone; because I am a man of unclean lips, and I dwell in the midst of a people of unclean lips: for mine eyes have seen the King, the Lord of hosts" (Isa. 6:5). In the presence of the Lord, this man found himself horizontal with the ground. That was the position Daniel took also. It was the position John took on the isle of Patmos: "And when I saw him, I fell at his feet as dead . . ." (Rev. 1:17).

What a picture of our holy God we have here! I must say that I stand merely on the fringe, thankful that I'm hidden in the cleft of the rock. Someday I am going to look upon the face of my Savior. I do not know what He looks like, but I am looking forward to that day.

CHAPTERS 2 AND 3

THEME: Ezekiel's call, preparation, and office as a watchman

EZEKIEL'S CALL

And he said unto me, Son of man, stand upon thy feet, and I will speak unto thee [Ezek. 2:1].

Apparently after the vision Ezekiel had seen, he was not standing up, but was down on his face. He will now receive a call and commission and an endowment with power for the office to which God has called him.

"Son of man"—God addresses him as "son of man." This title is found exactly one hundred times in the Book of Ezekiel. Daniel, also, is called the son of man. Only these two men in the Old Testament were called by this title. This is also the title that the Lord Jesus appropriated to Himself; eighty-six times in the New Testament He used this title for Himself. It speaks of Him in His rejection, His humiliation, and His exaltation; He is the Son of Man.

Ezekiel did pass through a great deal of suffering. If someone were to ask me whose position I would rather not have—Daniel's, Jeremiah's or Ezekiel's—I would say I would rather not have Ezekiel's. Certianly Daniel was in danger in the court of Babylon—just ask the lions down there in the den where Daniel spent a night with them! If God had not intervened, Daniel would have been lion food. But I would prefer his job to Ezekiel's because he at least had luxurious quarters there in the palace of the king of Babylon. Also, Jeremiah at this time was pretty much retired, although he had been in grave danger during his active ministry until the deportation of the people into captivity. However, this man Ezekiel was sent to do a hard job, a very difficult job. He had the job of speaking to an apostate people. He was sent to people who thought they were God's people, but actually they were in rebellion against God.

The Spirit of God now comes upon Ezekiel and prepares him for this office:

And the spirit entered into me when he spake unto me, and set me upon my feet, that I heard him that spake unto me [Ezek. 2:2].

The Spirit of God gave Ezekiel the power to do the job He had given him to do. I believe that when God calls you to do a job He will give you the power to do that job. In fact, God's work can *only* be done with the power of God. If God has called you to do a certain thing, He'll give you the power to do it. The best position you can come to is to recognize that you are not able in your own strength to do the job the Lord has given to you. Moses finaly came to the realization—after forty years in the wilderness—that he could not deliver the people. God said to him, "I can do it through you." God called him to deliver the people, and he was able to do it—not because there was anything in Moses, but because there was a great deal in God.

This is so practical for us today: it works in the ministry, in the pew, and on the mission field. A young couple once came to me saying they had been called to the mission field. I questioned them carefully because I frankly did not feel they were called, although I could not be sure and certainly did not want to stand in their way. They went to the mission field but came back a casualty. As I talked to them, I found they were bitter and felt that God had let them down. They had been willing to go, willing to be martyrs; yet God had not used them. I asked them, "Did it ever occur to you that if you had been called to the mission field, He would have given you the power to do the job?" They had never looked at it from that viewpoint. My friend, we need to recognize that, if we are called of God, He is going to give us the power to do the job. The important thing then is to make sure that we are truly called of God to do a certain thing.

Ezekiel was called to do a better job than any man I can think of. God is going to tell him about his job. I think that if God had told me something like this when I entered the ministry I would have said, "Now wait a minute, Lord, I'm handing in my resignation right now. I think I'll continue in my job as a bank clerk and see if I can work myself up in the banking world." I'm glad He didn't tell me what He told Ezekiel, because I must confess I am a coward and I come from a long line of cowards. I admire this man Ezekiel. Notice what God tells him about his job:

> **And he said unto me, Son of man, I send thee to the children of Israel, to a rebellious nation that hath rebelled against me: they and their fathers have transgressed against me, even unto this very day.**

> **For they are impudent children and stiffhearted. I do send thee unto them; and thou shalt say unto them, Thus saith the Lord God [Ezek. 2:3–4].**

This is a tremendous statement that God makes: "I am going to send you to these people—they are 'a rebellious nation.'" The word *rebellious* occurs again and again in the Book of Ezekiel. They are a people in rebellion against God.

The work that is translated "nation" is not the word that God generally used for His chosen people. The word in the Hebrew is *goi*, and it is the word that Israel used to speak of the Gentiles, the pagans, the heathen. What has happened is that Israel has sunk to the level of the heathen people who lived round about them. God says that they are "a rebellious nation"—they've rebelled against Him—and they are "impudent children."

My friend, the hardest people to reach with the gospel today are church members—those who are in church and who have rejected the gospel and rejected the Word of God. Although they are in church, they are actually against God. They think that being a Christian means to be nice little boys and girls. They play at church—it's a nice game for them. They seek to be sweet and to keep their noses clean. They want to live a life on the surface which is very sedate and comfortable. They don't want anyone coming in and telling them they are lost sinners who need to be saved and to become obedient to God. They are hard people to reach, and my heart goes out to my brethren who are in the ministry today—they are sitting on a hot seat. And I would counsel any young man who is considering the ministry to be sure about his call. If he is not sure of his call, maybe he should sell insurance or something else rather than go into the ministry. To be in the ministry today is not easy *if* you are going to stand for the Word of God.

> **And they, whether they will hear, or whether they will forbear, (for they are a rebellious house,) yet shall know that there hath been a prophet among them [Ezek. 2:5].**

God says to Ezekiel, "I am calling you to go to these people, and whether they hear you or whether they don't, they are going to know that there was a prophet of God among them—I'll make sure of that." After Ezekiel was gone, the people would say that he was certainly a prophet of God, although they disagreed with him.

I'll be frank with you. All I want after I'm gone is for people to say that I preached the Word of God the best I knew how. That is what is important.

> **And thou, son of man, be not afraid of them, neither be afraid of their words, though briers and thorns be with thee, and thou dost swell among scorpions: be not afraid of their words, nor be dismayed at their looks, though they be a rebellious house [Ezek. 2:6].**

Apparently Ezekiel was going to be in danger, but God says, "Be not afraid of them, neither be afraid of their words." The Lord really lays it on the line to Ezekiel just what his job was going to be like.

PREPARATION OF THE PROPHET

In chapter 3 we have the preparation of the prophet for a hard job, a difficult assignment. Jeremiah was a different type of individual from Ezekiel. Jeremiah was the prophet of the broken heart, tears often streaming from his eyes. At that crucial moment in history God needed Jeremiah to let His people know that it was breaking His heart to send them into captivity. Now the people have gone into captivity, and they are bitter and rebellious. However, at this time the temple had not yet been burned or the city of Jerusalem destroyed. It would not be until seven years after this delegation of captives arrived in Babylon that that destruction would occur. Therefore, the false prophets were still telling the people that they were God's people and they would go back home. They said to this man Ezekiel, "Who do you think you are to tell us these things? We are God's people, and we are going back to our land. We will not be in captivity a long time." But God had told Ezekiel, "You tell them they are *not* going back. They are going to be in captivity for seventy years just as Jeremiah said. They are going to be in Babylon seventy years, and they are going to work hard there along the canals, working in the fields and building buildings. It is going to be a hard lot for them."

Moreover he said unto me, son of man, eat that thou findest; eat this roll, and go speak unto the house of Israel [Ezek. 3:1].

"Son of man"—again, this is the title the Lord gives Ezekiel in this hard job, in the suffering he would experience.

"Eat that thou findest; eat this roll, and go speak unto the house of Israel." This is quite a diet—he is to eat the Word of God. The Word of God should become part of us, my friend. No man ought to preach the Word whose heart is not in it and who doesn't believe every word he says. Otherwise, he should get out of the ministry. The pulpit is no place for flowery speech and high-flown excess verbiage. The pulpit is the place to declare the Word of God.

So I opened my mouth, and he caused me to eat that roll.

And he said unto me, Son of man, cause thy belly to eat, and fill thy bowels with this roll that I give thee. Then did I eat it; and it was in my mouth as honey for sweetness [Ezek. 3:2–3].

For a good diet study the Word of God. May I ask you, do you love the person of Christ? Maybe I ought to first ask, do you love the Word of God? You will never love Him unless you love the Word of God.

A seminary professor asked me one time, "What *theory* of inspiration do you hold?" I said to him, "The theory I hold is no theory at all—*love the Book.*" You have to love the Word of God before it will ever become meaningful to you. The Word of God reveals a Person to you and then you fall in love with Him. Ezekiel said, "It was in my mouth as honey for sweetness"—he loved the Word of God.

> **And he said unto me, Son of man, go, get thee unto the house of Israel, and speak with my words unto them.**
>
> **For thou art not sent to a people of a strange speech and of an hard language, but to the house of Israel [Ezek. 3:4–5].**

Ezekiel was not sent to speak to foreigners but to his own people. He would not go as a missionary who has to learn a foreign tongue and a hard language—God sent him "to the house of Israel."

> **Not to many people of a strange speech and of an hard language, whose words thou canst not understand. Surely, had I sent thee to them, they would have hearkened unto thee.**
>
> **But the house of Israel will not hearken unto thee; for they will not hearken unto me: for all the house of Israel are impudent and hardhearted [Ezek. 3:6–7].**

"Ezekiel, I am sending you to a congregation that is impudent and in rebellion against Me. They won't hear Me, and they are not going to hear you either."

> **Behold, I have made thy face strong against their faces, and thy forehead strong against their foreheads.**

> **As an adamant harder than flint have I made thy fore-
> head: fear them not, neither be dismayed at their looks,
> though they be a rebellious house [Ezek. 3:8–9].**

The Lord tells Ezekiel, "You are to go ahead and give them My Word, and I am going to make your head hard." Now God didn't make Jeremiah's head hard. Jeremiah had a soft heart, and he couldn't stand up against all the trouble he faced. At one time he even went to the Lord and resigned. Ezekiel is not about to resign. God says, "The children of Israel are hardheaded, and I am going to make your head harder than theirs."

A man came to me one time and said, "You know, our preacher really talked hard to the board the other night, and I don't think a preacher ought to talk that way to the board." "Well," I said, "what kind of a board is it?" He replied, "They've caused the pastor a lot of trouble." I told him, "That's the kind of problem Ezekiel had, but God made his head harder than Israel's. I just hope your preacher's head is harder than anyone's on the board."

HIS OFFICE AS WATCHMAN

Now God tells Ezekiel what he is to do and how he is to warn Israel.

> **Then I came to them of the captivity at Tel-abib, that
> dwelt by the river of Chebar, and I sat where they sat,
> and remained there astonished among them seven days.**

> **And it came to pass at the end of seven days, that the
> word of the Lord came unto me, saying,**

> **Son of man, I have made thee a watchman unto the
> house of Israel: therefore hear the word at my mouth,
> and give them warning from me.**

> **When I say unto the wicked, Thou shalt surely die; and
> thou givest him not warning, nor speakest to warn the
> wicked from his wicked way, to save his life; the same**

wicked man shall die in his iniquity; but his blood will I require at thine hand.

Yet if thou warn the wicked, and he turn not from his wickedness, nor from his wicked way, he shall die in his iniquity; but thou hast delivered thy soul [Ezek. 3:15–19].

God gives to Ezekiel the job of being a watchman to warn His people. They may not want it, but he is to warn them. God says to him, "If you do not warn them that they are going to die in their sins, I am going to hold you responsible. However, if you warn them and they continue in their disobedience and die in their sins, you will not be responsible."

My friend, I would hate to be in the place of a minister who does not give out the Word of God. I'd hate to be in his position and stand before the Lord Jesus someday in judgment. A man who has the Word of God should have the intestinal fortitude to declare the Word of God. This was Ezekiel's responsibility, and God chose the right man for the job—he was as hard as a hickory nut.

The watchman held a very important position in the ancient world, in that day of walled cities. The cities were walled for protection, and the gates were closed at nightfall. A watchman then ascended the wall to begin the vigil of the long, dark night. With a trained eye he peered into the impenetrable darkness which surrounded the city. With a trained ear alert to every noise, he listened for the approach of danger, for the approach of an enemy.

The Word of God has quite a bit to say about the watchman. In Isaiah 62:6 we read: "I have set watchmen upon thy walls, O Jerusalem, which shall never hold their peace day nor night. . . ." And then in Psalm 127:1 it says, "Except the LORD build the house, they labour in vain that built it: except the LORD keep the city, the watchman waketh but in vain."

In the Hebrew culture, the watchmen functioned in three watches of the night; that is, they had three shifts: from dark until about midnight; from midnight until cockcrow, which was probably about two or three o'clock; and from then until dawn. The watchman in the morning watch was the one who announced the dawn. The Romans had the night divided into four watches.

We might think that the practice of having watchmen belongs to a backward age and a day that is past, that at the dawn of civilization it was satisfactory but it's not needed today. However, we are finding out again that we need watchmen. The police who patrol all during the night in our cities are watchmen. I personally feel they should have more support from the citizens and from the legal profession. We should stand behind them. I know that some of them individually are not what they should be, but we should respect their office and respect the fact that they do protect us during the night. But if we continue on the lawless path on which we are now, I am afraid that the day will come when they will not be able to help us at all.

The Book of Isaiah teaches us that the watchman had not only a responsibility, but also a visibility. He was to be able to distinguish the enemy out there in the darkness. Today, the minister is to be the watchman for his community. He should be able to give a warning of danger—he is *responsible* to give that type of message.

> **Again, When a righteous man doth turn from his righteousness, and commit iniquity, and I lay a stumblingblock before him, he shall die: because thou hast not given him warning, he shall die in his sin, and his righteousness which he hath done shall not be remembered; but his blood will I require at thine hand [Ezek. 3:20].**

This verse has been used to argue that a believer can fall from grace, a teaching which is not found in the Word of God. Galatians 5:4 is the only place where you will find the expression ". . . fallen from grace." There it is not speaking of salvation but of those who have been saved by grace but have fallen down to a legal level and are attempting to live by the law instead of living by grace. The great teaching of Galatians is that we are saved by grace and are to live by grace.

Here in Ezekiel we have a man who is living under the time of law. His life was determined by righteous acts. Under normal circumstances the righteous acts he might perform might look very good. But under time of stress and strain he might turn from God, and he would be judged for it. We are not to construe that he was once saved. He will be tested at the end of his life as to whether he is a child of God or not.

Today you and I are living under grace, and righteousness is determined in a little different way. We are constituted righteous by faith in Jesus Christ. We are saved by grace through faith. In Romans 4:5 we are told "But to him that worketh not, but believeth on him that justifieth the ungodly, his faith is counted [reckoned] for righteousness." The true believer today may fall into sin, but he will not deliberately practice and live in sin: "Whosoever is born of God doth not commit [practice] sin . . ." (1 John 3:9). If a believer falls into sin, a gracious provision is made—we have an Advocate with the Father, and we can come to Him in confession of our sins.

The emphasis in Ezekiel is not so much upon this man living under law but upon the responsibility of the watchman. The watchman is to warn the man who has turned from good works to living in a way that conforms to the standard of the enemy.

> **And the hand of the Lord was there upon me; and he said unto me, Arise, go forth into the plain, and I will there talk with thee [Ezek. 3:22].**

Having been told he is to be a watchman, God now tells Ezekiel to leave these people. For seven days he has sat among them overwhelmed by how far they have apostatized and turned from God. God calls him to leave them.

> **Then I arose, and went forth into the plain: and, behold, the glory of the Lord stood there, as the glory which I saw by the river of Chebar: and I fell on my face [Ezek. 3:23].**

The subject of the glory of God will appear again and again in the Book of Ezekiel. What is glory, by the way? Some will say that glory is something you cannot see, that it is intangible. I feel that is entirely wrong. Glory is something that produces a sensation on all five of our senses. Glory has size. How big is it? Is it long or square or round? May I say, glory has the size of the infinity of space. The Word of God tells us, "The heavens declare the glory of God; and the firmament sheweth his handiwork" (Ps. 19:1). The glory of God is seen in this tremendous universe that you and I live in. Glory also has a beauty to it: ". . . whose glorious beauty is a fading flower . . ." (Isa. 28:1). Glory is beautiful. My, heaven is going to be a beautiful place. How lovely it's going to be! Glory has to do with adornment. We read in Scripture that He was ". . . glorious in his apparel . . ." (Isa. 63:1). He is really dressed up and lovely in the garb that He wears. There is a majesty about glory. Psalm 8:1 declares, "O LORD our Lord, how excellent is thy name in all the earth! who hast set thy glory above the heavens." This is the majesty of God; it is bright and light, precious and pure. Finally, glory also sets forth honor and dignity. Daniel said, "O thou king, the most high God gave Nebuchadnezzar thy father a kingdom, and majesty, and glory, and honour" (Dan. 5:18). The very name of God suggests His dignity, His glory. Ezekiel saw the glory of the Lord.

> **Then the spirit entered into me, and set me upon my feet, and spake with me, and said unto me, Go shut thyself within thine house.**
>
> **But thou, O son of man, behold, they shall put bands upon thee, and shall bind thee with them, and thou shalt not go out among them [Ezek. 3:24–25].**

The usual interpretation of this verse is that the enemy binds Ezekiel so that they can take him out of the house. However, Ezekiel wanted to stay in that house, and he would not go although they had bound him.

Instead of speaking a great deal, Ezekiel is going to act out the parables which God gives to him. This is one of them: he goes into his house and locks himself in. Why? To show that God has rejected this rebellious people.

> **And I will make thy tongue cleave to the roof of thy mouth, that thou shalt be dumb, and shalt not be to them a reprover: for they are a rebellious house.**

But when I speak with thee, I will open thy mouth, and thou shalt say unto them, Thus saith the Lord GOD; He that heareth, let him hear; and he that forbeareth, let him forbear: for they are a rebellious house [Ezek. 3:26–27].

Ezekiel's job is to say, "Thus saith the Lord GOD." Back in chapter 2, verse 7 we read, "And thou shalt speak my words unto them." This man is to give God's Word to these people, and that is the only time he's to speak to them, He is to be dumb at other times. He had only the Word of God to give them.

CHAPTERS 4 AND 5

THEME: Judgment of Jerusalem; sign of the prophet shaving his hair

In chapters 4 and 5 Ezekiel is going to use certain signs and act out certain parables before the people. At this time Jerusalem was not yet destroyed, and the false prophets were telling the people of Israel that they were going to have peace. They were saying that the Jews already in Babylonian captivity would return to their land shortly, but Ezekiel is going to confirm the word of Jeremiah, who had told them they would not be going back and that Jerusalem would be destroyed.

G. K. Chesterton writing in the early twentieth century said, "This is the age of pacifism, but it is not the age of peace." Throughout history man has engaged in fifteen thousand wars and he has signed some eight thousand peace treaties; yet during five or six thousand years of history he has never enjoyed more than two to three hundred years of true peace. Man is a warlike creature, whether he likes to think so or not. Paul wrote in 1 Thessalonians 5:3, "For when they shall say, Peace and safety; then sudden destruction cometh upon them, as travail upon a woman with child; and they shall not escape." May I say to you, there is only one Prince of Peace, the Lord Jesus Christ.

JUDGMENT OF JERUSALEM

Ezekiel is going to show these people that there is not going to be any peace and that Jerusalem is going to be destroyed.

> **Thou also, son of man, take thee a tile, and lay it before thee, and portray upon it the city, even Jerusalem [Ezek. 4:1].**

"A tile" in that day meant a brick. This was their writing material; the Babylonians used clay bricks on which they kept their records. Many,

many of these bricks have been found, and they have writing upon them. They are almost square, about fourteen by twelve inches in size.

What Ezekiel was to do was to draw the city of Jerusalem on the brick (I do not know just how he did it), and then he was to break the brick to show that the city was going to be destroyed.

> **Moreover take thou unto thee an iron pan, and set it for a wall of iron between thee and the city: and set thy face against it, and it shall be besieged, and thou shalt lay siege against it. This shall be a sign to the house of Israel [Ezek. 4:3].**

Now Ezekiel was to take an iron pan and put it between himself and this picture of Jerusalem which he had made to show that God had put a wall between Himself and the city of Jerusalem. The destruction of the city was inevitable; it could not be stopped. What a tremendous way in which to bring God's message to these people!

The sign of the tile portrayed the siege of Jerusalem. The second sign of the pan showed the hardships of divine judgment, that the people were to go through terrible suffering. A third sign describes additional punishments to come upon Jerusalem. It is the sign of the defiled bread:

> **Take thou also unto thee wheat, and barley, and beans, and lentils, and millet, and fitches, and put them in one vessel, and make thee bread thereto, according to the number of the days that thou shalt lie upon thy side, three hundred and ninety days shalt thou eat thereof.**

> **And thy meat which thou shalt eat shall be by weight, twenty shekels a day: from time to time shalt thou eat it.**

> **Thou shalt drink also water by measure, the sixth part of an hin: from time to time shalt thou drink.**

> **And thou shalt eat it as barley cakes, and thou shalt bake it with dung that cometh out of man, in their sight.**

> And the LORD said, Even thus shall the children of Israel
> eat their defiled bread among the Gentiles, whither I
> will drive them [Ezek. 4:9–13].

These instructions would be overwhelming to most of us, but they
were especially difficult for Ezekiel to follow because he was a priest
and had never eaten anything unclean:

> Then said I, Ah Lord GOD! behold, my soul hath not
> been polluted: for from my youth up even till now have I
> not eaten of that which dieth of itself, or is torn in
> pieces; neither came there abominable flesh into my
> mouth [Ezek. 4:14].

However, this was to be a sign from the Lord of the famine the people
would experience at the time of the destruction of the city of Jerusalem. Despite the continued promises of the false prophets, the city
and the people were going to be lost. These various signs described
the horrors that were to come.

SIGN OF THE PROPHET SHAVING HIS HAIR

Chapter 5 opens with Ezekiel acting out yet another sign to the
people:

> And thou, son of man, take thee a sharp knife, take thee
> a barber's razor, and cause it to pass upon thine head
> and upon thy beard: then take thee balances to weigh,
> and divide the hair.
>
> Thou shalt burn with fire a third part in the midst of the
> city, when the days of the siege are fulfilled: and thou
> shalt take a third part, and smite about it with a knife:
> and a third part thou shalt scatter in the wind; and I
> will draw out a sword after them.
>
> Thou shalt also take thereof a few in number, and bind
> them in thy skirts [Ezek. 5:1–3].

This must have looked something like one of our modern commercials for an electric razor—only they didn't have electric razors in those days! Just what was the meaning of this? Ezekiel was to shave his head and his beard, which was unusual for a priest to do. I imagine the people gathered all around to watch as Ezekiel shaved himself out there in the open.

After he shaved, Ezekiel carefully divided the hair into three parts. One third of the hair he took and burned inside the city. This represented the people who were going to be beseiged and burned with fire inside the city at the time of its destruction—this is exactly what happened to them. The second third of the hair he took and smote—he really worked it over. This depicted what was to happen to those people who lived through the seige—they fell by the sword. The last third of the people were scattered out; this group included those who went down to Egypt taking Jeremiah with them. The small remnant of God's people who eventually returned to the city is pictured by the few hairs that were bound up in Ezekiel's skirts.

> **A third part of thee shall die with the pestilence, and with famine shall they be consumed in the midst of thee: and a third part shall fall by the sword round about thee; and I will scatter a third part into all the winds, and I will draw out a sword after them [Ezek. 5:12].**

This is the message that Ezekiel brought, and he made its meaning very clear.

> **So will I send upon you famine and evil beasts, and they shall bereave thee; and pestilence and blood shall pass through thee; and I will bring the sword upon thee. I the LORD have spoken it [Ezek. 5:17].**

Ezekiel's warning to the people went unheeded. The destruction of Jerusalem and the suffering endured by the people should be a warning to us of the reality of divine judgment. But we are so far removed from it, and very few people are really acquainted with the Word of

God today. (The greatest sin among Christians is ignorance of the Word of God.) God gave this warning to the people of Jerusalem, but it has a message for us also, as does all Scripture. My friend, when the judgment of God begins, it is going to be too late to make your decision. Today, if you will hear His voice, He says, "(. . . behold, *now* is the accepted time; behold, *now* is the day of salvation.)" (2 Cor. 6:2, italics mine). The real "Now Generation" are those who have not postponed their decision but have already accepted God's salvation.

CHAPTER 6

THEME: Sword to fall upon Jerusalem; remnant to be saved

The Book of Ezekiel is a very orderly book, and up to this point we have had prophecies which largely concerned Jerusalem. However, the prophet will now turn his attention to the whole land of Israel: judgment is going to come upon the whole land.

Ezekiel is with the second delegation of people who were taken captive by Nebuchadnezzar. They were slaves of the government of Babylon working in the agricultural area by the river Chebar, the great canal running off the Euphrates River. Most of the people, however, were still back in the land, and Jerusalem had not yet been devastated. The false prophets continued to assure the people that everything was going to be all right and that the captives would be able to return shortly. Meanwhile, Jeremiah was saying that the captivity would last seventy years, but they paid no attention to him. They listened to the false prophets because their message sounded better and was very optimistic.

I have found the same attitude among people throughout the years of my ministry. After I preached a series of messages on the judgments of God found in the books of the prophets, one very prominent man in my church at that time withdrew from the church. He said, "I go to church to be comforted, and I am not being comforted." He did not want to hear the Word of God. I discovered later that in his business dealings he did not need to be comforted; the judgment messages were good for him—they were digging in right where he was! Another lady stopped coming to my church, saying, "There were times when Dr. McGee made me feel very bad. Now I go to church, and the preacher makes me feel very good." Frankly, her church was a cult, and its message concerned how to make friends and influence people. It emphasized the power of positive thinking: just feel good about it, and it will be good. May I say to you, that is *not* the message of the Word of God.

In chapters 6 and 7 we have two messages of judgment. Ezekiel now is going to speak on that which concerns all of the land, and his message is that the idolators are to die and the land is to be desolated.

SWORD TO FALL UPON JERUSALEM

And the word of the LORD came unto me, saying [Ezek. 6:1].

This verse opens the first of the two messages; the second message in chapter 7 begins the same way: "Moreover the word of the LORD came unto me, saying" (Ezek. 7:1). The people would not accept what Ezekiel said, but Ezekiel told them, "I'm not telling you what I *think*, and I'm not telling you what I *hope* or what I'd *like* to see come to pass. I'm telling you what *God* says."

It is also interesting to note that both of these messages conclude with "and they shall know that I am the LORD." God sent this judgment upon them so that they would know He was the Lord; one of the purposes of judgment is that men might know that God is a holy God.

This world needs to know that God is a holy God. We have had a great deal of emphasis upon the fact that God is love. While it is true that God is love, it is only half the story. We need to look on the other side on the coin: God is holy, and God *will* punish sin. If you turn in disobedience from Him, if you deny Him and do not accept His salvation, there is only one alternative left—judgment. Men today try to excuse themselves; they do not want to recognize that they are sinners. They attempt to write God off and bow Him out of His universe by saying He does not even exist.

A brilliant young Hebrew, who was a chaplain at the University of Pittsburgh a number of years ago, attempted to show that God did not exist. His argument was based on the premise that the God of the Hebrew Bible is depicted as the faithful protector of His chosen people, but at least six million Jews had died at the hands of the Nazis. He wrote, "To believe in the God of the covenant today you must affirm that their Creator [that is, of the nation Israel] used Adolph Hitler as the rod of His wrath to send His people to the death camps, and I find myself utterly incapable of believing this. Even the existentialist's leap of faith cannot resurrect this dead God after Auschwitz." This young rabbi speaks of the death of God as a cultural event. Wistfully and sadly he comes to the conclusion that there is no God because the God of the covenant is a God who would protect Israel and would never let anything happen to them. May I point out that he never takes into consideration, as Ezekiel did, that there might be something wrong with the people upon whom the judgment came. They had turned their backs upon God and had denied Him. They had been given a special privilege, and that privilege created a responsibility which they did not measure up to.

Ezekiel is telling the people that it is God who is sending this judgment that He might confirm to them that He is a *holy* God. His judgment is an awful thing. Paul wrote, "Knowing therefore the terror of the Lord, we persuade men . . ." (2 Cor. 5:11). Because Ezekiel was made aware of God's holiness at the beginning of his ministry, he devoted his life to the ministry of "persuading men."

> **Son of man, set thy face toward the mountains of Israel, and prophesy against them [Ezek. 6:2].**

The judgment is to come upon the entire land.

> **And say, Ye mountains of Israel, hear the word of the Lord God; Thus saith the Lord God to the mountains, and to the hills, to the rivers, and to the valleys; Behold, I, even I, will bring a sword upon you, and I will destroy your high places [Ezek. 6:3].**

"Mountain" in Scripture, if used figuratively, speaks of government, but you need to determine if it is being used literally or figuratively. I believe Ezekiel is speaking of that land, the good old terra firma— right down where there's plenty of dirt.

"I will destroy your high places." In that land under every kind of tree there was a heathen altar around which the grossest immorality took place. This is what the heathen, the Gentiles did, but now this nation, God's chosen people, had given themselves over to the same idolatry. God says to them, "Judgment is coming upon you."

> **And your altars shall be desolate, and your images shall be broken: and I will cast down your slain men before your idols.**

> **And I will lay the dead carcases of the children of Israel before their idols; and I will scatter your bones round about your altars [Ezek. 6:4–5].**

It is too bad that the Jews in Germany did not read the Book of Ezekiel rather than turning to a man like Hitler, which the entire nation did at the beginning. Israel should have turned to the living and true God and been acquainted with His method of dealing with men. You cannot trifle with God, my friend. Judgment does come.

America struggles to bring peace to the world; but, instead of solving our problems, they continue to mount up. Why? Because God judges. Do you think God is a senile old man with long whiskers, sitting on a cloud and weeping crocodile tears? My friend, God is a holy God. In chapter 1 Ezekiel saw a vision of a holy God: those wheels within wheels depicting the energy of God as He moves forward to accomplish His purposes, and the fire and whirlwind showing that God does move in judgment upon this earth in which we live. To understand God in this way may be a bitter pill, but when we take the bitter pills the doctor gives us, they do help us. We need to swallow this bitter pill: we are dealing with a holy God, and He is not wrong; we are the ones who are wrong. Are you willing to admit that?

God is saying, "I am going to judge Israel, and it is not going to be easy." I am afraid Israel was not at all willing to admit their wrong.

REMNANT TO BE SAVED

> **Yet will I leave a remnant, that ye may have some that shall escape the sword among the nations, when ye shall be scattered through the countries [Ezek. 6:8].**

There were some among these people who remained faithful to God. The nation as a whole went away from God, but there was a believing remnant. This is true of the church today. Liberalism has taken over the bulk of the organized church, but there are many of God's people left. God takes note of the faithful ones.

And they that escape of you shall remember me among the nations whither they shall be carried captives, because I am broken with their whorish heart, which hath departed from me, and with their eyes, which go a-whoring after their idols: and they shall loathe themselves for the evils which they have committed in all their abominations [Ezek. 6:9].

"And they that escape of you shall remember me among the nations whither they shall be carried captives." What is this remnant going to do? They are going to be a witness for God.

"Because I am broken with their whorish heart, which hath departed from me" would be better translated "when I shall have broken their whorish heart which has departed from me." They are people who belong to Him, but they have played the harlot, they have committed spiritual adultery. The organized church which will remain after Christ takes His true church out of the world is also called a harlot in Revelation 17. That is the most frightful chapter in the Word of God—it presents a terrible picture.

"They shall loathe themselves for the evils which they have committed in all their abominations." This was one of the results of judgment, but we do not see this result in our world today. This means simply that there will be more judgment, and that judgment is coming during the Great Tribulation period. The people at that time will gnaw their tongues because of the judgment of God. You would think there would be a great wave of repentance, but there will not be among that crowd.

In Ezekiel's day there were those who loathed themselves—they repented because they were still close to God. That will be true of

God's people always. If you do not hate yourself whenever you serve
the Devil, then you must not be one of God's people.

> **And they shall know that I am the LORD, and that I have
> not said in vain that I would do this evil unto them
> [Ezek. 6:10].**

"And they shall know that I am the LORD"—this is said three times in
this chapter, and it is another result of judgment. Again, we do not see
this result happening in our own day. Instead of recognizing the hand
of God, people are saying that He is not even there. They argue that if
He did exist, He would always help them. Oh, my friend, where do we
get that idea? God is judging sin. People rebel against this; they do not
want a God who judges. You can make a God after your own likeness
if you want to, but the holy God is still out there. You might wish He
would go away, but He is not going to go away. He will continue to
judge.

> **Then shall ye know that I am the LORD, when their slain
> men shall be among their idols round about their altars,
> upon every high hill, in all the tops of the mountains,
> and under every green tree, and under every thick oak,
> the place where they did offer sweet savour to all their
> idols [Ezek. 6:13].**

I happen to know that the persecution under Hitler drove many wonderful Jews to God. There is a great company of believers today in
Europe as a result of that. We forget about them, and very little is said
about them. I received a letter once from a wonderful girl whose par-
ents died in those gas chambers, and she testified to the fact that the
horrible experience had been the means of her salvation. We need to
recognize the hand of God—He is a holy God. If He did not spare His
own Son, but let Him die when He became sin for us, why in the
world do sinners think they will escape His judgment?

"Their altars, upon every high hill"—God spells out the reason He
judged them in the land. My friend, the judgment of God is still upon

that land. Many folk like to speak of it as "the land of milk and honey." Don't kid yourself—it is not the land of milk and honey today. The people are not turning to Him, and His judgment is still on that land.

So will I stretch out my hand upon them, and make the land desolate, yea, more desolate than the wilderness toward Diblath, in all their habitations: and they shall know that I am the Lord [Ezek. 6:14].

I do not know about "the wilderness toward Diblath," but I do know what it is like between Jerusalem and Jericho right now, and I am not interested in buying real estate there. If it were not for their need of protection, I think Israel would be willing to turn it back to the Arabs and let them have it!

"They shall know that I am the Lord"—again, this is one of His tremendous purposes in judgment.

CHAPTER 7

THEME: Prophecy of the final destruction of Jerusalem

Chapter 7 contains the second of two messages of judgment against the entire land of Israel. Through chapter 5 Ezekiel's messages had concerned Jerusalem, but now the whole land is in view. Jerusalem had not yet been destroyed and, although most of the inhabitants had been removed from the land, many people still remained there. However, the events which had already taken place did not cause them to turn to God.

Moreover the word of the LORD came unto me, saying [Ezek. 7:1].

Ezekiel is passing on to the people of Israel what God has to say. The first message, given in chapter 6, opened with the same words.

Also, thou son of man, thus saith the Lord GOD unto the land of Israel; An end, the end is come upon the four corners of the land [Ezek. 7:2].

Judgment was to come upon that land, and of course it would include the people of the land. The land of Israel and the nation Israel are always considered together in the Word of God.

A new element is added to Ezekiel's prophecy in this message—this is now the prophecy of the *final* destruction of the land and of Jerusalem. The final deportation will take place, and the city will be destroyed.

Now is the end come upon thee, and I send mine anger upon thee, and will judge thee according to thy ways, and will recompense upon thee all thine abominations [Ezek. 7:3].

This message is in the form of marvelous Hebrew poetry, and throughout this chapter I would like to quote to you a translation by the late Dr. A. C. Gaebelein (*The Prophet Ezekiel*, p. 48). He has translated this quite literally in poetic form. This then is his translation of verses 1–3.

> And the Word of Jehovah came unto me, saying, And thou Son of Man, thus saith Jehovah unto the land of Israel:
>
> An end cometh! The end
> Upon the four corners of the land.
> Now cometh the end upon thee
> And I will send mine anger upon thee,
> And I will judge thee according to thy ways,
> And I will bring upon thee all thine abominations.

God says to Israel, "I am going to judge you according to your ways." The judgment or the punishment will fit the crime.

We need to ask ourselves: How serious is it to be a professed witness for God and yet really be a phony? How serious is it to be a church member and not be saved? That brings the issue right down to where the rubber meets the road for us in this day. I have said many times that I would rather be a Hottentot in the darkest corner of Africa, bowing down to an idol, than to be a church member sitting in the pew, professing to be a Christian, yet not knowing the Lord Jesus Christ as my Savior! I will not argue with you about what God will do with the Hottentot—the Lord has His plan for him. I will talk about church members who are not truly saved. That is the issue in our day which corresponds to what Ezekiel is talking about. Ezekiel says that such a man's responsibility is great, because he has heard the Word of God, and he has turned his back upon it. The more he hears, the greater his responsibility grows, I can assure you of that.

And mine eye shall not spare thee, neither will I have pity: but I will recompense thy ways upon thee, and

thine abominations shall be in the midst of thee: and ye shall know that I am the LORD.

Thus saith the Lord GOD; An evil, an only evil, behold, is come.

An end is come, the end is come: it watcheth for thee; behold, it is come.

The morning is come unto thee, O thou that dwellest in the land: the time is come, the day of trouble is near, and not the sounding again of the mountains.

Now will I shortly pour out of my fury upon thee, and accomplish mine anger upon thee: and I will judge thee according to thy ways, and will recompense thee for all thine abominations.

And mine eye shall not spare, neither will I have pity: I will recompense thee according to thy ways, and thine abominations that are in the midst of thee; and ye shall know that I am the LORD that smiteth [Ezek. 7:4–9].

Again, let me give you Dr. Gaebelein's translation of these verses (The Prophet Ezekiel, p. 48):

And mine eyes shall not spare thee,
Neither will I have pity:
Because I will bring thy ways upon thee
And thine abominations shall be in the midst of thee:
And ye shall know that I am Jehovah.

Thus saith the Lord Jehovah!
An evil—an only evil!—behold it cometh.
An end is come—the end is come!
It awaketh against thee. Behold it cometh!
O inhabitant of the land, thy doom is come unto thee
The set time is come, the day is near,

The day of tumult.
And not the joyous shouting upon the mountains:
Now will I soon pour out my fury upon thee

And accomplish mine anger against thee.
I will judge thee according to thy ways,
And I will bring upon thee all thine abominations.
Mine eye shall not spare, neither will I have pity.
According to thy ways will I render unto thee,
And thine abominations shall be in the midst of thee,
And ye shall know that I am Jehovah, who smiteth.

This is a tremendous passage of Scripture which, I dare say, few deal with today—it is totally unknown to multitudes of church members. Someone will argue, "Well, it belongs way back in the Old Testament and that makes it different." My friend, Ezekiel's language is tame compared to the Book of Revelation and to the words of the Lord Jesus in Matthew 25. Ezekiel's words here are those of a sissy compared to many passages in the New Testament. The God of the New Testament is the same Person as the God of the Old Testament, and He will punish sin in any age.

I mentioned in the previous chapter a young Jewish rabbi who wants to dismiss God altogether because he cannot reconcile what happened to the six million Jews in Hitler's Germany. All I want to say is that ought to be a warning to the church of God today. Will God judge? Yes, He will! It is no wonder that Paul said, "Knowing therefore the terror of the Lord, we persuade men . . ." (2 Cor. 5:11).

Many are playing church today, making it a cheap sort of thing. They speak of their "allegiance," their "dedication, but do not have a full commitment to Jesus Christ. That is the tragedy of this moment. Our problem is not that we do not have enough church members—the problem is we have too many who are not genuine Christians. There was a great preacher in New York City many years ago who made this statement: "One cold church member hurts the cause of Christ more than twenty blatant, blaspheming atheists." Ezekiel's message was not popular in his day, nor is it today.

Behold the day, behold, it is come; the morning is gone forth; the rod hath blossomed, pride hath budded.

Violence is risen up into a rod of wickedness: none of them shall remain, nor of their multitude, nor of any of theirs: neither shall there be wailing for them.

The time is come, the day draweth near: let not the buyer rejoice, nor the seller mourn: for wrath is upon all the multitude thereof.

For the seller shall not return to that which is sold, although they were yet alive: for the vision is touching the whole multitude thereof, which shall not return; neither shall any strengthen himself in the iniquity of his life.

They have blown the trumpet, even to make all ready; but none goeth to the battle: for my wrath is upon all the multitude thereof [Ezek. 7:10–14].

Here is Dr. Gaebelein's rendering of this passage (*The Prophet Ezekiel*, pp. 49–50):

Behold the Day! Behold it cometh!
Thy doom advanceth:
The rod hath blossomed, pride hath budded.
Violence has risen up into a rod of wickedness;
None of them shall remain; yea none of their multitude
Nor their wealth; neither shall there be eminency among them.
The time is come, the day draweth near;
Let not the buyer rejoice, nor the seller mourn,
For wrath is upon all the multitude thereof.
For the seller shall not return to that which is sold,
Even though he were yet amongst the living.
In the vision touching the whole multitude thereof
It shall not be revoked;
And none shall through his iniquity assure his life.

They have blown the trumpet and made all ready,
But none goeth to the battle;
For my wrath is upon all the multitude thereof.

The thing that characterized these people was that they were a bunch of protesters—they were pacifists and wouldn't go to war. They refused to stand for that which was right, my friend. The judgment came, and when the enemy came in, he didn't have any silly notions about pacifism. I mentioned before G. K. Chesterton's comment, "This is the age of pacifism, but it is not the age of peace." It is true that men today are weary of war, but as long as there is iniquity in the human heart God has said, "There is no peace . . . to the wicked" (Isa. 57:21). Isaiah repeated that truth three times in his prophecy.

They shall cast their silver in the streets, and their gold shall be removed: their silver and their gold shall not be able to deliver them in the day of the wrath of the LORD: they shall not satisfy their souls, neither fill their bowels: because it is the stumblingblock of their iniquity [Ezek. 7:19].

Dr. Gaebelein's translation is (*The Prophet Ezekiel*, p. 51):

They shall cast their silver in the streets,
And their gold shall be as an unclean thing;
Their silver and their gold shall not be able to deliver them
In the day of Jehovah's wrath;
They cannot satisfy their souls, neither fill their bowels,
Because it was the stumbling block of their iniquity.

Too often in America we have felt that the almighty dollar could solve every problem of life. We have spent billions of dollars throughout the world in pursuit of peace. We haven't done a very good job, but we sure have spent a lot of money. It is very comfortable to have a few dollars on hand, but they will not solve life's problems. This is what

God is saying here to the people of Israel who felt that their accumulated wealth would protect them—it did not.

> **As for the beauty of his ornament, he set it in majesty: but they made the images of their abominations and of their detestable things therein: therefore have I set it far from them.**
>
> **And I will give it into the hands of the strangers for a prey, and to the wicked of the earth for a spoil; and they shall pollute it.**
>
> **My face will I turn also from them, and they shall pollute my secret place: for the robbers shall enter into it, and defile it [Ezek. 7:20–22].**

Dr. Gaebelein continues on page 51:

> And the beauty of their ornaments, they turned it to pride,
> And the images of their abominations, their detestable things made they of it.
> And I shall give it to the hands of strangers for a prey,
> And to the wicked of the earth for a spoil; and they shall profane it.
> For I will turn my face from them.
> And they shall defile my secret place,
> And robbers shall enter into it and profane it.

This is an awesome description of the judgment of God, but if you want to read something even more awesome and which still lies ahead for the world, read Revelation 18 and 19, which describe the destruction of commerical Babylon. It speaks of a day in which men trust in big business and the stock market and depend on the success of Fifth Avenue. It is a day in which the boys in grey flannel suits make business successful, and the government assures that everything in life will go all right. But it wasn't all right, and it didn't save them. When they needed deliverance, it could not deliver them.

Make a chain: for the land is full of bloody crimes, and the city is full of violence.

Wherefore I will bring the worst of the heathen, and they shall possess their houses: I will also make the pomp of the strong to cease; and their holy places shall be defiled [Ezek. 7:23–24].

These verses are translated on page 51 by Dr. Gaebelein for us:

Form a chain,
For the land is full of bloody crimes,
And the city full of violence.
Therefore will I bring the worst of the nations,
And they shall possess their houses;
And I will make the pride of the mighty to cease,
And there sanctuaries shall be defiled.

"The land is full of bloody crimes, and the city is full of violence"—what an accurate picture of our own day!

"Wherefore I will bring the worst of the heathen, and they shall possess their houses." There are many today who want to believe that God will never permit Russia to destroy America. Where do we get that idea? God permitted Babylon, a pagan nation, to destroy His own people. Can America come down? People will say, "Oh, no. We are sending missionaries. We are such nice, lovely people." My friend, it is not safe to walk the streets of America. There's violence; there's crime. Until a nation will become a law-abiding people, God cannot bless them.

You see, people do not like to read Ezekiel's message; they would rather read John 14. Don't misunderstand me—I love John 14, too. But we must remember that Ezekiel 7 is in the Bible also. I do not know where we got the idea that one chapter was a little bit more important than another to read. We need to at least give Ezekiel 7 equal time and let him present his case.

CHAPTER 8

THEME: Vision of the glory; temple destroyed because of defilement

We now come to the second major section of the prophecy of Ezekiel. In this division of the book the complete captivity of Jerusalem and Israel will become a reality, and the glory of the Lord will depart from the temple in Jerusalem.

VISION OF THE GLORY

In chapter 8 Ezekiel has another vision of the glory of the Lord. The vision transports Ezekiel to Jerusalem, and God's glory appears in the temple at Jerusalem. The question always arises: Was Ezekiel *actually* transported to Jerusalem? I will give you my viewpoint, but this is an issue on which no one can be dogmatic and on which few agree. One answer to the question is that Ezekiel simply saw a vision and he saw it there by the river Chebar. A second explanation is given that Ezekiel literally went to Jerusalem and walked around and saw all that he records here. I do not accept either of these interpretations.

I believe that Ezekiel's experience was very similar to the experiences that the apostles Paul and John had. Paul said that he had been caught up to the third heaven (2 Cor. 12:1–3). It is my feeling that that occurred at the time he was stoned in Lystra in the Galatian country and was left for dead. I believe he actually was dead and that God raised him from the dead, and that at that time he was caught up to the third heaven. John also, as recorded in Revelation 4, was caught up into heaven. In this I feel John is a picture of the Rapture of the church, in which all true believers will be caught up to be with the Lord. Chapters 2 and 3 of Revelation frequently mention "the church," but after John's experience in chapter 4, the church (the "called-out body") is no longer mentioned. She is now the "bride" of Christ, the church which is no longer on the earth but is with her Lord. Therefore, I see John's being caught up into heaven as a picture of the Rapture.

Ezekiel was actually caught up as Paul and John were, but I do not think that the people at Jerusalem and of the surrounding area were aware that he was there. We are not dealing with the natural, and I cannot offer you a natural explanation. God caught him up, and what happened was supernatural.

> **And it came to pass in the sixth year, in the sixth month, in the fifth day of the month, as I sat in mine house, and the elders of Judah sat before me, that the hand of the Lord GOD fell there upon me [Ezek. 8:1].**

Ezekiel was sitting among the elders. I imagine it was a pretty doleful crowd there.

> **Then I beheld, and lo a likeness as the appearance of fire: from the appearance of his loins even downward, fire; and from his loins even upward, as the appearance of brightness, as the colour of amber [Ezek. 8:2].**

This is very similar to a part of Ezekiel's vision recorded in chapter 1. That tremendous vision of the glory of God is the basis of every vision in the Book of Ezekiel, and I personally think it is the basis of the Book of Revelation.

> **And he put forth the form of an hand, and took me by a lock of mine head; and the spirit lifted me up between the earth and the heaven, and brought me in the visions of God to Jerusalem, to the door of the inner gate that looketh toward the north; where was the seat of the image of jealousy, which provoketh to jealousy.**

> **And behold, the glory of the God of Israel was there, according to the vision that I saw in the plain [Ezek. 8:3–4].**

"And he put forth the form of an hand." God is a Spirit; He doesn't have a hand like I have. But when the Scripture tells me that the *fingerwork* of God is in the heavens then I am able to understand, because I could not understand how God could make the world without a hand. Scripture uses our own finite terms to aid our understanding of the infinite.

"And he took me by a lock of mine head." You will remember that Ezekiel had shaved himself—his face and his head—but that had been about a year before this, and his hair has had time to grow out. God took him by the hair of his head.

"And the spirit lifted me up between the earth and the heaven, and brought me in the visions of God to Jerusalem." Ezekiel was actually caught up and removed by the Spirit of God to Jerusalem. Whether or not his body went along with him is a point I will not argue about, but I rather think it did. Ezekiel's withdrawal to Jerusalem is not something new in Scripture. Elijah also was caught up (2 Kings 2), and in the New Testament we read of Philip: "And when they were come up out of the water, the Spirit of the Lord caught away Philip, that the eunuch saw him no more: and he went on his way rejoicing" (Acts 8:39). Philip was removed bodily, and that is exactly what happened to Elijah and possibly to this man Ezekiel.

"To Jerusalem, to the door of the inner gate that looketh toward the north; where was the seat of the image of jealousy, which provoketh to jealousy." I believe this "image of jealousy" may be a reference to the idol which Manasseh put in the temple (see 2 Kings 21; 2 Chron. 33) which was an abomination and a blasphemy. Perhaps that old idol had been pushed into a corner and forgotten for awhile, but now in Ezekiel's day it has been pulled out, and the people who should have turned to God in repentance are again worshiping that idol.

In chapters 8–10 of Ezekiel we are going to see the gradual withdrawal of the glory of the Lord from the temple and from Israel. I feel that the glory actually departed back during the reign of Manasseh and that Ezekiel is given a vision of that here. I know that most expositors of Scripture feel that the glory left at the time of the Captivity, but I do not feel that is accurate. If the glory did not leave during the exceedingly evil reign of Manasseh, I cannot see any other period in

Israel's history which would cause the glory, the presence of God, to leave.

In this chapter we do not have the complete vision of the departure of the glory. Here we see the glory, and then, because the people did not turn back to God, the glory lifted up from the temple and went out over the city to the east and waited there. It will not be until chapter 10 that we will see the final departure of the glory.

I do not think there is any evidence after the reign of Manasseh that the glory of the Lord was in the temple. This vision was given to Ezekiel to show that God is merciful. He was loath to leave and was ready to save the people of Israel if they would turn to Him. God is merciful, and God is love. But He is also a righteous and just God who cannot permit evil in His universe. He cannot permit that which is contrary to Himself.

Today, God cannot save us by our righteousness or our perfection—we have none to present to Him. He cannot accept anything less than righteousness. He therefore had to provide a redemption for man, and we must come His way through faith in the Lord Jesus Christ. If we do not, we have an old nature that is in rebellion against God, and God is not going to permit that in His universe, any more than a policeman should harbor a criminal in his home.

TEMPLE DESTROYED BECAUSE OF DEFILEMENT

Then said he unto me, Son of man, lift up thine eyes now the way toward the north. So I lifted up mine eyes the way toward the north, and behold northward at the gate of the altar this image of jealousy in the entry [Ezek. 8:5].

The temple is defiled. The people are no longer worshiping the living and true God but are breaking the first two commandments.

And he brought me to the door of the court; and when I looked, behold a hole in the wall.

> **Then said he unto me, Son of man, dig now in the wall: and when I had digged in the wall, behold a door.**
>
> **And he said unto me, Go in, and behold the wicked abominations that they do here [Ezek. 8:7–9].**

If Ezekiel is over there just in his spirit, how in the world could he crawl through a hole? How does a spirit dig a hole? If he were a spirit, he wouldn't *need* to dig a hole. I believe he was there bodily, and he dug a hole and was apparently brought down into a basement or a cave. What does he find down there?

> **So I went in and saw; and behold every form of creeping things, and abominable beasts, and all the idols of the house of Israel, portrayed upon the wall round about [Ezek. 8:10].**

These people are worshiping the creature rather than the Creator—this is as low as they could go. Man will turn to this type of thing when he has absolutely repudiated the living and true God. This is what they were doing in Egypt at the time of the Exodus; they were worshiping every kind of beast. That is the reason the plagues upon Egypt were aimed at the different gods of Egypt. In Romans 1 we read: "Because that, when they knew God, they glorified him not as God. . . . Who changed the truth of God into a lie, and worshipped and served the creature more than the Creator, who is blessed for ever . . ." (Rom. 1:21, 25). This means that Israel has sunk down to the level of the nations round about her, and she is no longer a witness for the living and true God. For this reason, He will destroy the temple.

> **And there stood before them seventy men of the ancients of the house of Israel, and in the midst of them stood Jaazaniah the son of Shaphan, with every man his censer in his hand; and a thick cloud of incense went up.**
>
> **Then said he unto me, Son of man, hast thou seen what the ancients of the house of Israel do in the dark, every**

> man in the chambers of his imagery? for they say, The
> LORD seeth us not; the LORD hath forsaken the earth
> [Ezek. 8:11–12].

You see, they have dismissed God. They said He was not watching
them. And those today who say that God is dead are really trying to
say that God is not looking at us, that we are not responsible to Him,
we owe Him nothing and may do as we please. That is what Israel was
doing. They were apparently worshiping this idol, and they were doing it in secret. Talk about a secret lodge—they sure had one in the
temple there.

My friend, in this day the believer's *body* is God's temple on earth.
Is He pleased by what He sees going on in our minds and hearts?

> He said also unto me, Turn thee yet again, and thou
> shalt see greater abominations that they do.

> Then he brought me to the door of the gate of the LORD's
> house which was toward the north; and, behold, there
> sat women weeping for Tammuz.

> Then said he unto me, Hast thou seen this, O son of
> man? turn thee yet again, and thou shalt see greater
> abominations than these [Ezek. 8:13–15].

"There sat women weeping for Tammuz." This was an awful thing
that was going on. Tammuz was the Babylonian Dumuzi, the god of
spring vegetation. He died in the fall and winter and went down to the
netherworld to be revived again each returning summer. The worship
of this god was practiced in Phoenicia and spread to Greece, where
Adonis was Tammuz' counterpart. These weeping women were cele-
brating the death of this god; his worship was actually the worship of
nature and connected with it were some vile and immoral ceremonies.

> And he brought me into the inner court of the LORD's
> house, and, behold, at the door of the temple of the LORD,

> **between the porch and the altar, were about five and twenty men, with their backs toward the temple of the LORD, and their faces toward the east; and they worshipped the sun toward the east [Ezek. 8:16].**

The greatest of all the abominations was the worship of the sun. This was happening right in the temple between the porch and the altar. They can sink no lower than this.

> **Then he said unto me, Hast thou seen this, O son of man? Is it a light thing to the house of Judah that they commit the abominations which they commit here? for they have filled the land with violence, and have returned to provoke me to anger: and, lo, they put the branch to their nose [Ezek. 8:17].**

"And, lo, they put the branch to their nose." There are many ways of interpreting this; Jewish commentators of the past have said that it speaks of shocking, low, and degrading religious rites. Perhaps it could be compared with a man "thumbing his nose" today. This is what they were doing to God!

God now expresses His anger—

> **Therefore will I also deal in fury: mine eye shall not spare, neither will I have pity: and though they cry in mine ears with a loud voice, yet will I not hear them [Ezek. 8:18].**

Israel has stepped over the line—they can go no lower than this. God will now judge them.

My friend, God loves you and will save you if you will come to Him by faith and trust Christ as your Savior. God also judges, and He is a holy and righteous God, and He makes no apology for it. We can say with Paul, ". . . Is there unrighteousness with God? God forbid" (Rom. 9:14). God is right in everything He does; if He judges, He is right to do so. It will be quite a revelation to this generation when it is shown that it is wrong and God is right. God will judge sin.

CHAPTERS 9 AND 10

THEME: Shekinah glory prepares to leave temple; Shekinah glory fills the holy place; Shekinah glory departs

SHEKINAH GLORY PREPARES TO LEAVE THE TEMPLE

In chapter 9 the Shekinah glory prepares to leave the temple at Jerusalem. I believe that from the days of Manasseh there was the coming and going of the Shekinah glory. God is merciful; He doesn't, in a petulant mood, give up on people. God is long-suffering and not willing that any should perish.

And, behold, six men came from the way of the higher gate, which lieth toward the north, and every man a slaughter weapon in his hand; and one man among them was clothed with linen, with a writer's inkhorn by his side: and they went in, and stood beside the brasen altar.

And the glory of the God of Israel was gone up from the cherub, whereupon he was, to the threshold of the house. And he called to the man clothed with linen, which had the writer's inkhorn by his side [Ezek. 9:2–3].

"Six men came from the way of the higher gate." These six men are angels—I see no other explanation for them. Angels are used by God in the judgment of this world. They are associated with the nation Israel and have nothing to do with the church. On the Day of Pentecost the Holy Spirit came—*not* angels—and when the Lord Jesus Christ comes to take the church out of the world, there will be no angels with Him. However, when He comes to the earth to establish His Kingdom, He will send forth His angels. We read in Matthew 13:41, "The Son of man shall send forth his angels, and they shall gather out of his kingdom all the things that offend, and them which do iniquity." Then in Matthew 16:27: "For the Son of man shall come in the glory of his Father with his angels; and then he shall reward every man according to his works." Finally, Paul wrote: "And to you who are troubled rest with us, when the Lord Jesus shall be revealed from heaven with his mighty angels, in flaming fire taking vengeance on them that know not God, and that obey not the gospel of our Lord Jesus Christ" (2 Thess. 1:7–8). After the third chapter in Revelation, there is no mention of the church which had been previously mentioned frequently. Why? The church is gone from the earth, and *angels* have taken over the judgment upon the earth.

"And the glory of the God of Israel was gone up from the cherub." That is, it had gone up from the Holy Place. The "cherub" were above the mercy seat. This is where the glory had been, but now it lifts up. The glory was a token of the presence of God, and it is now departing.

> **And the Lord said unto him, Go through the midst of the city, through the midst of Jerusalem, and set a mark upon the foreheads of the men that sigh and that cry for all the abominations that be done in the midst thereof [Ezek. 9:4].**

God has said, "Mark out the men who want these abominations and are seeking after them. I am going to judge them." But this man with the inkhorn marks out those "that sigh and that cry for all the abominations." These are the remnant which God will save in that city.

> **Then said he unto me, The iniquity of the house of Israel and Judah is exceeding great, and the land is full of blood, and the city full of perverseness: for they say, The Lord hath forsaken the earth, and the Lord seeth not [Ezek. 9:9].**

It was as if the people were saying, "God is blind, and He can't make it to the earth." That is the same as those who say today that God is dead.

It may be easy to say that God is not out there and He doesn't know what is going on in the earth, but when you really think about it, it is absurd. My friend, just because you haven't seen God and have seen no evidence of Him is no proof that He does not exist. I have never been to Tokyo, Japan, but I believe there is a great city by the name of Tokyo in Japan. I have never been there, and I can act as if it's not there, but the fact remains that it does exist. Just because a man has had no intimate relationship with God does not mean that God does not exist. The people of Israel were trying to say that God had forsaken the earth. Why? Because they had forsaken God.

And as for me also, mine eye shall not spare, neither will I have pity, but I will recompense their way upon their head [Ezek. 9:10].

The destruction of Jerusalem at the hands of Nebuchadnezzar and the burning of the temple were frightful things. Why did God do it? He has said, "I will recompense their way upon their head." God is running things, my friend; and, if you are out of step with Him, it might be well to get in step with Him. If I saw a lion coming down the street toward me, I wouldn't meet him head on. I would turn and be going the same direction as he was going as far ahead of him as I could go! You can defy God if you want to, but may I say to you, the chariot of the Lord is riding triumphantly, and God have mercy on you if you get in His way.

And, behold, the man clothed with linen, which had the inkhorn by his side, reported the matter, saying, I have done as thou hast commanded me [Ezek. 9:11].

There were those who were picked out for judgment, and there was the remnant which was to be saved. Our God is merciful when men will turn to Him; that fact makes His judgment actually more frightful.

SHEKINAH GLORY FILLS THE HOLY PLACE

In chapter 10 we continue Ezekiel's vision of the departing glory of the Lord. God has supernaturally transported Ezekiel to Jerusalem to let him see these things and then return to report to the major portion of the people of Israel who were already in captivity in Babylon. They were being told there by the false prophets that everything was fine in Jerusalem and they would return there shortly. Ezekiel will be able to go back and tell them why God is going to destroy the city and permit judgment to come upon them. We saw in chapter 8 that there was sufficient proof of the sin in the life of the people in Jerusalem—God made that evident to Ezekiel.

We need to see the fact that God judges; it is one of the evidences we have of the living God. We do not get by with our sin, and the very fact that we don't get by with it is proof that God exists. The "wheels within wheels" which Ezekiel saw speak of the energy of God as He moves in the affairs of men.

The glory of the Lord was above the cherubim—between the cherubim in the Holy of Holies in the temple. The nation of Israel had what no other nation had and, indeed, that which the church does not have today: the visible presence of God. In the ninth chapter of Romans, Paul lists about eight different points of identification which were unique to the nation of Israel, and one of them was "the glory." These people had the Shekinah glory, the visible presence of God, that which Ezekiel saw in his vision in the first chapter.

The glory began its departure in the previous chapter and will now continue to depart. It moved out from the temple and hovered over it. Now we read:

> **Then I looked, and, behold, in the firmament that was above the head of the cherubims there appeared over them as it were a sapphire stone, as the appearance of the likeness of a throne.**

> **And he spake unto the man clothed with linen, and said, Go in between the wheels, even under the cherub,**

and fill thine hand with coals of fire from between the cherubims, and scatter them over the city. And he went in in my sight [Ezek. 10:1–2].

The man clothed with linen is to scatter these coals from off the altar. The blood of the sacrifice was taken from the altar and put on the mercy seat. These coals speak of judgment. The people had refused the grace and mercy and redemption of God; now they must bear the judgment.

It is just as simple as this: God sent His Son because He loves you. Because He is holy, He had to pay the penalty for your sin and mine; He had to die on the cross. Christ is the propitiation, He is the mercy seat for our sins—not for ours only, but for the sins of the whole world. There is a mercy seat which you can come to, but if you reject it, the judgment of God must come upon you. Christ bore your judgment, and that is the only way God forgives you. It is not because you are a sweet little boy or a nice little Pollyanna glad-girl. You are a sinner and in rebellion against Him. The best that Christians can say today is that we are *saved* sinners; we are not superior people at all.

Judgment is now going to come to Jerusalem, the city that is the center of the earth. It is the very navel of the earth—that is what God calls it. It will be the center of the millennial kingdom, and it will be the eternal center of the earth. It is today the most sensitive piece of real estate on topside of the earth. Someone has put it like this: "Palestine because the nerve-center of the earth in the days of Abraham. Later on, the country became the truth-center because of Moses and the prophets. Ultimately, it became the salvation-center by the manifestation of Christ. His rejection led to its becoming the storm-center, as it has continued to be throughout many centuries. The Scriptures predict that it is to be the peace-center under the messianic kingdom, and it will be the glory-center in a new universe yet to be experienced." We are seeing through the vision of Ezekiel the departure of the glory from that city, but God has an eternal purpose in this city.

Then the glory of the LORD went up from the cherub, and stood over the threshold of the house; and the house was

filled with the cloud, and the court was full of the brightness of the LORD's glory [Ezek. 10:4].

The Shekinah glory had been confined to the Holy Place, the place which denoted the approach of these people to God. However, now the glory leaves the Holy Place there between the cherubim and hovers over the temple to see if the people will return to God.

And the sound of the cherubim's wings was heard even to the outer court, as the voice of the Almighty God when he speaketh.

And it came to pass, that when he had commanded the man clothed with linen, saying, Take fire from between the wheels, from between the cherubims; then he went in, and stood beside the wheels.

And one cherub stretched forth his hand from between the cherubims unto the fire that was between the cherubims, and took thereof, and put it into the hands of him that was clothed with linen: who took it, and went out.

And there appeared in the cherubims the form of a man's hand under their wings [Ezek. 10:5–8].

Again, this "hand" denotes the activity of God in performing certain things. "The heavens declare the glory of God; and the firmament sheweth his handiwork [actually, *fingerwork*]" (Ps. 19:1). The universe is the fingerwork of God, but God's work in His redemption of man was greater than that in creation. Isaiah said, "Who hath believed our report? and to whom is the *arm* of the LORD revealed?" (Isa. 53:1, italics mine). He used His *bared* arm. The only way that I can understand the work of God is to use terms with which I am acquainted. I use my *fingers* to do certain things, my *hands* to do other tasks, and my *arms* to do even heavier tasks. The greatest thing God has done is to perform the wonderful redemptive love act at the cross of Christ— that was His bared arm; but when God created the universe, He just used His fingers, or, as John Wesley put it: "God created the universe and didn't even half try." Ezekiel says here that the *hand* of God is moving in judgment.

> And when I looked, behold the four wheels by the cherubims, one wheel by one cherub, and another wheel by another cherub: and the appearance of the wheels was as the colour of a beryl stone [Ezek. 10:9].

Have you ever watched a wheel when it is going around? There's that flashing light, you know, like that of a precious stone. These wheels are in ceaseless activity and speak of the fact that God is busy. The Lord Jesus said, ". . . My Father worketh hitherto, and I work" (John 5:17). The Lord Jesus has been very busy on our behalf ever since He ascended back to heaven.

> And as for their appearances, they four had one likeness, as if a wheel had been in the midst of a wheel.
>
> When they went, they went upon their four sides; they turned not as they went, but to the place whither the head looked they followed it; they turned not as they went [Ezek. 10:10–11].

God has never had to come back to pick up something He has forgotten. He doesn't need to deviate from one side to the other; He never detours. He goes straight forward today toward the accomplishment of His purpose in the world.

> And their whole body, and their backs, and their hands, and their wings, and the wheels, were full of eyes round about, even the wheels that they four had.
>
> As for the wheels, it was cried unto them in my hearing, O wheel.
>
> And every one had four faces: the first face was the face of a cherub, and the second face was the face of a man,

> **and the third the face of a lion, and the fourth the face of
> an eagle [Ezek. 10:12–14].**

This, of course, is highly figurative, and I do not want to press this
point, but I believe we have the messages of the four Gospels set before
us. In the face of the eagle is pictured the *deity* of Christ—that's John's
Gospel. In the face of the lion is pictured the *kingship* of Christ, the
lion of the tribe of Judah—that's Matthew's Gospel. In the face of the
man is pictured the *humanity* of Christ—that's Luke's Gospel. Finally,
the face of the cherub (sometimes it is the ox) pictures the *servanthood*
of Christ—that's Mark's Gospel. He shed His blood that you and I
might have eternal life—He made a mercy seat. In the temple the cherubim looked down upon the blood of the sacrifice.

> **And the cherubims were lifted up. This is the living
> creature that I saw by the river of Chebar [Ezek. 10:15].**

Ezekiel refers to his first vision recorded in chapter 1.

THE GLORY LEAVES THE TEMPLE

> **Then the glory of the LORD departed from off the threshold of the house, and stood over the cherubims [Ezek.
> 10:18].**

The glory of the Lord lifts up from the temple.

> **And the cherubims lifted up their wings, and mounted
> up from the earth in my sight: when they went out, the
> wheels also were beside them, and every one stood at
> the door of the east gate of the LORD's house; and the
> glory of the God of Israel was over them above [Ezek.
> 10:19].**

The cherubim mounted up, and the glory moved out and stood at the
east gate.

> This is the living creature that I saw under the God of Israel by the river of Chebar; and I knew that they were the cherubims.
>
> Every one had four faces apiece, and every one four wings; and the likeness of the hands of a man was under their wings.
>
> And the likeness of their faces was the same faces which I saw by the river of Chebar, their appearances and themselves: they went every one straight forward [Ezek. 10:20–22].

I believe this vision pictures the fact that God would become incarnate, or, as John put it, "And the Word was made flesh . . ." (John 1:14).

CHAPTERS 11—13

THEME: Prophecy against Jerusalem's rulers; Ezekiel's enacting Jerusalem's destruction; prophecy against pseudoprophets, prophetesses

In chapter 11 there is a prophecy against the rulers who were still in Jerusalem. Although most of the people had been carried into captivity, Jerusalem had not yet been destroyed. Zedekiah was still on the throne. Not only were the rulers in rebellion against God, they were in rebellion against the king of Babylon, Nebuchadnezzar.

> **Moreover the spirit lifted me up, and brought me unto the east gate of the Lord's house, which looketh eastward: and behold at the door of the gate five and twenty men; among whom I saw Jaazaniah the son of Azur, and Pelatiah the son of Benaiah, princes of the people [Ezek. 11:1].**

Specific individuals are named who were princes of the people.

> **Then said he unto me, Son of man, these are the men that devise mischief, and give wicked counsel in this city:**
>
> **Which say, It is not near; let us build houses: this city is the caldron, and we be the flesh [Ezek. 11:2-3].**

In other words, these rulers were saying, "This city is our cup of tea—it's ours now. Most everybody has left, and we are going to continue. We're going to have peace and plenty and prosperity." Theirs was materialism of the worst sort.

> **Therefore prophesy against them, prophesy, O son of man.**

And the spirit of the Lord fell upon me, and said unto me, Speak; Thus saith the Lord; Thus have ye said, O house of Israel: for I know the things that come into your mind, every one of them [Ezek. 11:4-5].

God knows even what we are thinking. He knows our thoughts afar off.

Ye have multiplied your slain in this city, and ye have filled the streets thereof with the slain [Ezek. 11:6].

Apparently the rulers have slain those who stood for God.

Ye shall fall by the sword; I will judge you in the border of Israel; and ye shall know that I am the Lord [Ezek. 11:10].

God's purpose in judgment is that the people might know Him.

This city shall not be your caldron, neither shall ye be the flesh in the midst thereof; but I will judge you in the border of Israel [Ezek. 11:11].

God says that He is going to judge them.

Again the word of the Lord came unto me, saying,

Son of man, thy brethren, even thy brethren, the men of thy kindred, and all the house of Israel wholly, are they unto whom the inhabitants of Jerusalem have said, Get you far from the Lord: unto us is this land given in possession.

Therefore say, Thus saith the Lord God; Although I have cast them far off among the heathen, and although I have scattered them among the countries, yet will I be to them as a little sanctuary in the countries where they shall come [Ezek. 11:14-16].

God says, "There will be a remnant who will see Me. When they do, I'm going to be a little temple, a little sanctuary, and they will be able to approach Me." This was God's arrangement during the time the temple was destroyed. Daniel and many others were among those who sought the LORD during this period.

> **Therefore say, Thus saith the Lord GOD; I will even gather you from the people, and assemble you out of the countries where ye have been scattered, and I will give you the land of Israel.**
>
> **And they shall come thither, and they shall take away all the detestable things thereof and all the abominations thereof from thence.**
>
> **And I will give them one heart, and I will put a new spirit within you; and I will take the stony heart out of their flesh, and will give them an heart of flesh:**
>
> **That they may walk in my statutes, and keep mine ordinances, and do them: and they shall be my people, and I will be their God [Ezek. 11:17–20].**

God would return the people to the land. Who was it that came back? Those who were seeking God. There were less than 60,000 in the remnant which returned at the end of the seventy-year captivity.

> **But as for them whose heart walketh after the heart of their detestable things and their abominations, I will recompense their way upon their own heads, saith the Lord GOD [Ezek. 11:21].**

The judgment of God is coming. It is a great tragedy today that the ministry ignores the fact that judgment is coming upon this earth. God's judgment is one of the sure proofs of His existence.

> Then did the cherubims lift up their wings, and the wheels beside them; and the glory of the God of Israel was over them above.

> And the glory of the LORD went up from the midst of the city, and stood upon the mountain which is on the east side of the city [Ezek. 11:22–23].

The glory of the Lord moves from Jerusalem out to the Mount of Olives east of the city.

> Afterwards the spirit took me up, and brought me in a vision by the spirit of God into Chaldea, to them of the captivity. So the vision that I had seen went up from me [Ezek. 11:24].

Ezekiel is brought back to Babylon where he began.

> Then I spake unto them of the captivity all the things that the LORD had shewed me [Ezek. 11:25].

He returns to tell the people that the false prophets have lied to them. He has seen the vision—Jerusalem will be destroyed, and full captivity is near at hand. He will be able to tell them why God will judge them. The people are not going to listen to Ezekiel, but he is to continue to be a sign unto them.

EZEKIEL'S ENACTING JERUSALEM'S DESTRUCTION

Chapter 12 opens a section in which Ezekiel continues to proclaim that judgment is imminent, but the people will not believe. The important thing here is the proclamation of the Word of God; Ezekiel is to make sure that he gives the Word of God—

> The word of the LORD also came unto me, saying [Ezek. 12:1].

Five times in this chapter (vv. 1, 8, 17, 21, and 26), Ezekiel says, "The word of the LORD came unto me, saying." Do you get the impression that Ezekiel is trying to tell these people that he is giving them the Word of the Lord? He is giving them nothing short of that.

Son of man, thou dwellest in the midst of a rebellious house, which have eyes to see, and see not; they have ears to hear, and hear not: for they are a rebellious house [Ezek. 12:2].

Of course, God had warned Ezekiel before about these people, but He is reminding him because Ezekiel may get discouraged. God said way back at the beginning of Israel's history, "Yet the LORD hath not given you an heart to perceive, and eyes to see, and ears to hear, unto this day" (Deut. 29:4). These people had their eyes closed and their ears stopped. Ezekiel was not the only prophet who confirmed this truth about these people—Isaiah (Isa. 6:9–10) and Jeremiah (Jer. 5:21) did also. In addition, the Book of Acts closes with this statement: "Saying, Go unto this people, and say, Hearing ye shall hear, and shall not understand; and seeing ye shall see, and not perceive: For the heart of this people is waxed gross, and their ears are dull of hearing, and their eyes have they closed; lest they should see with their eyes, and hear with their ears, and understand with their heart, and should be converted, and I should heal them" (Acts 28:26–27). These people had closed eyes and ears.

Today, when people say they cannot believe, it is not a mental problem; it is a matter of the will of the heart—they do not *want* to believe. Some say they have certain "mental reservations," mental hurdles which they cannot get over. My friend, your mind is not big enough to take even one little hurdle. The problem is never in the mind but in the will. There is sin in the life, and a man does not want to turn to God; he does not want to believe Him.

Israel is just a miniature of the world; that is, the condition of Israel described here is the condition of the world today. In her spirit of unbelief she was a little microcosm of the entire world. That is why we need to look carefully at what the Book of Ezekiel has to say.

I remember talking to a college professor who told me that he appreciated my ministry and what I had to say about the Bible, but that he had certain mental reservations. I had to bite my tongue—I do not believe he was so far ahead of me intellectually that he could see so much more than I! You know what his real problem was? He was having an affair with a former student from one of his classes. *She* was his "intellectual problem"—he did not want to forsake the sin in his life. Blindness in part had happened in Israel, and this is true of our world today.

Because of Israel's unbelief, Ezekiel is not only going to give the people a parable, he is actually going to act it out. Ezekiel was a very brilliant man, but I think he also had a real sense of humor. I would love to have seen his face when he went through some of these mechanics! I think he might have been somewhat of a ham actor and been greatly amused as he did these things.

> **Therefore, thou son of man, prepare thee stuff for removing, and remove by day in their sight; and thou shalt remove from thy place to another place in their sight: it may be they will consider, though they be a rebellious house.**

> **Then shalt thou bring forth thy stuff by day in their sight, as stuff for removing: and thou shalt go forth at even in their sight, as they that go forth into captivity.**

> **Dig thou through the wall in their sight, and carry out thereby.**

> **In their sight shalt thou bear it upon thy shoulders, and carry it forth in the twilight: thou shalt cover thy face, that thou see not the ground: for I have set thee for a sign unto the house of Israel [Ezek. 12:3-6].**

I tell you, this is a good one! Here's what Ezekiel does: He goes into his house (the houses then were right on the street, by the way); he packs his baggage like he's going on a trip, digs through the wall, and comes up out in the street. You can imagine the effect that would have—a man coming out through the wall bringing his suitcases with him! People would *have* to stop and look.

Here in Pasadena, California, where I live, digging up the street is not anything new. Actually, the city here plays a game with all of us. They dig up one street, and so you decide to get smart and use another street. So the next day they find out what new street you're using, and then they go dig up that street too! It gets to be quite a puzzle, like a maze, finding your way around dug-up streets. But I have a notion that when this man Ezekiel came up in the middle of the street with his suitcase, it was something new, and people stopped to ask, "Where are you going? What's the big idea?" Ezekiel had an answer for them:

> **And in the morning came the word of the LORD unto me, saying,**
>
> **Son of man, hath not the house of Israel, the rebellious house, said unto thee, What doest thou?**
>
> **Say thou unto them, Thus saith the Lord GOD; This burden concerneth the prince in Jerusalem, and all the house of Israel that are among them.**
>
> **Say, I am your sign: like as I have done, so shall it be done unto them: they shall remove and go into captivity.**
>
> **And the prince that is among them shall bear upon his shoulder in the twilight, and shall go forth: they shall dig through the wall to carry out thereby: he shall cover his face, that he see not the ground with his eyes [Ezek. 12:8–12].**

Zedekiah was on the throne in Jerusalem, and the false prophets were saying to the captives, "Look, Nebuchadnezzar has made two sieges of Jerusalem, and he's carried away captives, but he did not destroy the city, he did not burn the temple, and he did not execute the king.

You are going to be able to return soon. There's nothing to worry about." But Ezekiel says, "I have news for you: What I have just done is a picture of what is happening back in Jerusalem. The king over there, the prince (that's Zedekiah), thinks he's very clever. He thinks he will be able to slip out of the city during the siege, but he won't. When he leaves the city, he won't even see the ground."

Do you know why Zedekiah didn't see the ground? Read the historical record in 2 Kings 25:1–7; Nebuchadnezzar put out his eyes. Zedekiah was a deceptive, wicked fellow, and he had broken his treaty with Nebuchadnezzar. Nebuchadnezzar, the pagan king, was more honorable than the man on Israel's throne. There is nothing that hurts the church more today than a dishonest Christian, particularly when it is a layman who is active in the Lord's work but in the business world has a poor reputation. Zedekiah was like that, and Ezekiel's message was a bitter pill for those captives to swallow when the false prophets had said, "It's so wonderful back in Jerusalem."

Moreover the word of the LORD came to me, saying,

Son of man, eat thy bread with quaking, and drink thy water with trembling and with carefulness;

And say unto the people of the land, Thus saith the Lord GOD of the inhabitants of Jerusalem, and of the land of Israel; They shall eat their bread with carefulness, and drink their water with astonishment, that her land may be desolate from all that is therein, because of the violence of all them that dwell therein [Ezek. 12:17–19].

This is quite a stunt Ezekiel is going to pull. He is to bring his table out into the street and sit there, trembling as he eats. Then the people will come and say, "What's the matter with you? Have you got a chill, or is it something you ate?" Ezekiel will give them God's message: "I want you to know what's happening over yonder in Jerusalem. There's a famine over there. There's fear over there. God is destroying the city." What an awesome message he has to bring.

> Son of man, what is that proverb that ye have in the land
> of Israel, saying, The days are prolonged, and every vi-
> sion faileth?
>
> Tell them therefore, Thus saith the Lord GOD; I will
> make this proverb to cease, and they shall no more use it
> as a proverb in Israel; but say unto them, The days are at
> hand, and the effect of every vision [Ezek. 12:22–23].

Ezekiel is saying, "God has been patient, but it's all up now. The captivity is coming, and God is not going to wait any longer."

> Therefore say unto them, Thus saith the Lord GOD;
> There shall none of my words be prolonged any more,
> but the word which I have spoken shall be done, saith
> the Lord GOD [Ezek. 12:28].

Everybody wants to believe that the future out yonder is beautiful. My
friend, the only beautiful thing that lies ahead is the fact that someday
the Lord Jesus will take His church out of the world—that is the only
hope we have. This world is not going to get better, and we are not
going to have peace. In all of recorded history there have only been
two to three hundred years of what could actually be called peace—
man is not building the new world he thinks he is.

PROPHECY AGAINST PSEUDO PROPHETS
AND PROPHETESSES

In chapter 13 we have the prophecy against the false prophets, the
pseudo prophets and prophetesses. Notice that the women were also
getting involved in this. Have you ever noticed how many cults and
isms have been founded by women or how women play a very prominent part in them? It may not be popular to say that, but it was true in
Ezekiel's day and it is true in ours.

Ezekiel continues to give the Word of the Lord:

And the word of the LORD came unto me, saying,

Son of man, prophesy against the prophets of Israel that prophesy, and say thou unto them that prophesy out of their own hearts, Hear ye the word of the LORD;

Thus saith the Lord GOD; Woe unto the foolish prophets, that follow their own spirit, and have seen nothing! [Ezek. 13:1–3].

What was the problem? These prophets prophesied "out of their own hearts." God have mercy on the man who stands in the pulpit and gives his own viewpoints and does not give the Word of God. Now it is possible to make a mistake in interpretation, and I have sometimes made mistakes. However, let me make it clear that I am attempting to interpret the *Word of God*. These men were merely giving what they thought: how to make friends, influence people, think positively, be self-reliant, and think of yourself as a wonderful individual, not as a sinner. This was their message: "Everything is all right in Jerusalem."

Likewise, thou son of man, set thy face against the daughters of thy people, which prophesy out of their own heart; and prophesy thou against them,

And say, Thus saith the Lord GOD; Woe to the women that sew pillows to all armholes, and make kerchiefs upon the head of every stature to hunt souls! Will ye hunt the souls of my people, and will ye save the souls alive that come unto you? [Ezek. 13:17–18].

Ezekiel is to resist the false prophetesses—"Set thy face against the daughters of thy people . . . and prophesy thou against them."

In Genesis 10:8–9, Nimrod is called a mighty hunter before the Lord. Actually, he was a hunter of the souls of men. That is also what these false cults do—they hunt out the souls of men.

The women were involved in this also. In 2 Peter 2:1 Peter said, "But there were false prophets also among the people [that is, Israel], even as there shall be false teachers among you, who privily shall bring in damnable heresies, even denying the Lord that bought them, and bring upon themselves swift destruction." Today we have many women who are involved in spiritualism with its mediums and fortune tellers and necromancers and witches. There are quite a few in Southern California—I always thought we had them, but now they openly claim they are witches.

"Woe to the women that sew pillows to all armholes." What these women were doing was giving out amulets, a little something to put on your arm, to keep you from getting sick or to protect you from harm. "And make kerchiefs upon the head of every stature to hunt souls!" They give you a handkerchief which they have prayed over, and it will help you get well (as if there were merit in that rather than in the Lord)! My friend, what you see about you today is *not* new. It is as old as the human race. When Ezekiel clearly denounced it in his day, it was "the word of the LORD," not his own word.

CHAPTERS 14—16

THEME: Prophecy against the elders' idolatry; vision of the vine; Jerusalem likened to an abandoned baby adopted by God

Chapter 14 is divided into two major sections: the prophecy against the idolatry of the elders and the certainty of the destruction of Jerusalem. Both sections open with, "The word of the LORD came unto me" (vv. 2, 12). The Lord continues in this chapter to outline why He judged the city of Jerusalem as He did. The principles that are put down here are operative today also. God still judges nations.

PROPHECY AGAINST THE ELDERS' IDOLATRY

In these verses Ezekiel will call the elders of Israel to repent. I have noticed throughout both the Old and New Testaments *repentance* is God's message to His own people, those who profess to belong to Him. "Repent and turn to God"—that will be Ezekiel's message here.

> **Then came certain of the elders of Israel unto me, and sat before me [Ezek. 14:1].**

The elders come to Ezekiel, and oh, how pious these fellows are! They pretend they want to listen to the prophet. It is like coming to church with a big Bible under your arm, pretending you want to serve the Lord.

> **And the word of the LORD came unto me, saying,**
>
> **Son of man, these men have set up their idols in their heart, and put the stumblingblock of their iniquity before their face: should I be inquired of at all by them? [Ezek. 14:2–3].**

In effect the elders say, "Oh, brother Ezekiel, we don't worship idols!" It was true they had not made idols, but the Lord said, "These men have set up their idols in their heart."

Samson was also a man who pretended to be God's man, and the Spirit of God *did* come upon him at times. The Holy Spirit—never his hair—was the secret of his power. But there came a day when he went out and ". . . he wist it not . . ." (Lev. 5:17)—he knew not that the Spirit of God had departed from him. He had kept toying and playing with sin and at the same time wanting to be God's man. How many people today in the church keep toying and playing with sin and think they are getting by with it? My friend, they are *not* getting by with it. Judgment is inevitable. They may go through the form and ritual of religion, keeping up a false front, but they actually have idols in their hearts.

Ezekiel is told by the Lord that these men are phonies. They pretend they want to hear his message, but they do not hear it at all. When he turns around, they will put a knife in his back.

> **Therefore speak unto them, and say unto them, Thus saith the Lord God; Every man of the house of Israel that setteth up his idols in his heart, and putteth the stumblingblock of his iniquity before his face, and cometh to the prophet; I the Lord will answer him that cometh according to the multitude of his idols [Ezek. 14:4].**

God says He will judge these men. The Lord Jesus called the religious rulers of His day *hypocrites*. He used that frightful, awful word more than anyone. Ezekiel is speaking to the spiritual leaders of the people. How tragic this is! God is going to judge them. God will always judge phony religion. I believe that whenever a church or an individual departs from the truth, God will judge.

> **Therefore say unto the house of Israel, Thus saith the Lord God; Repent, and turn yourselves from your idols;**

**and turn away your faces from all your abominations
[Ezek. 14:6].**

God has laid it on the line that these men are phonies, not genuine,
having idols in their hearts, sin in their hearts. Again, someone might
say about Samson, "My, isn't that terrible about Samson! I'd hate to
live like that man did and have that judgment come upon me." However, I am afraid that there are folk who sit in the church pew and yet
would like to live in sin, to taste the fruits of sin. The very thing they
condemn outwardly is the thing in their heart they would like to do.
This old nature we have is bad, but God says, "Repent. Come to Me."
He is gracious to Israel. He is giving them an opportunity to become
genuine, but they will not.

CERTAIN DESTRUCTION OF JERUSALEM

The false prophets were still running around saying, "God will spare
Jerusalem. It is His city—He loves it. He says His eye is there." They
could quote an abundance of Scripture about it. It is possible to quote
an isolated Scripture or two to support false doctrine today. However,
you cannot take a verse here and there; you must look at the whole
picture presented in Scripture. When you do, you will not be able to
support false theories. These prophets were wrong, and God is saying
very explicitly that Jerusalem is to be judged.

The word of the LORD came again to me, saying,

**Son of man, when the land sinneth against me by tres-
passing grievously, then will I stretch out mine hand
upon it, and will break the staff of the bread thereof,
and will send famine upon it, and will cut off man and
beast from it [Ezek. 14:12–13].**

God says to Ezekiel, "The city is a rebellious city which has continu-
ously rebelled against Me. I have given them opportunity to return to
Me, and they will not."

God is very definite, and He means what He says. Judgment is unavoidable. Listen to just how serious He is:

> **Though these three men, Noah, Daniel, and Job, were in
> it, they should deliver but their own souls by their righteousness, saith the Lord GOD [Ezek. 14:14].**

If Noah were in the city of Jerusalem, the Lord says, they would not listen to him. Just imagine what a warning Noah would have been to those people! But the people in Noah's day did not listen to him, and the people of Jerusalem would not have listened to him had he been there.

I get rather amused over the excitement about the search for Noah's ark. I think they may find it, but let me ask you: How many believers do you think its discovery will make? If Noah himself were here today, who would believe him? They would call him a square and an old fogey! (One thing nice about being a square is that you don't go around in circles as do a lot of other people. Some of those going around in circles really think they are big wheels, too!)

They wouldn't have listened to Noah, and they wouldn't have listened to Daniel. Nebuchadnezzar listened to Daniel, however. What a tribute that is to Daniel! Yonder in the palace of the world's first great ruler, Nebuchadnezzar, is Daniel. The Babylonians knew Daniel, and they knew he was God's man. The Lord says that the Israelites would not have listened to Noah or Daniel or Job!

> **Or if I bring a sword upon that land, and say, Sword, go
> through the land; so that I cut off man and beast from it
> [Ezek. 14:17].**

God says that He intends to bring a sword upon the land. He is going to allow Nebuchadnezzar into the land, and he will destroy it.

> **Though Noah, Daniel, and Job, were in it, as I live, saith
> the Lord GOD, they shall deliver neither son nor daugh-**

ter; they shall but deliver their own souls by their righteousness [Ezek. 14:20].

Noah would not have been able to save his own family in that city—
"they shall but deliver their own souls by their righteousness." Daniel
saved a couple of empires, but if he had been in that city he could not
have helped them at all. That is the reason that God got Daniel out of
Jerusalem. God's people wouldn't hear him, but an old pagan king in
Babylon listened to Daniel and made him prime minister.

How many churches are there today where the people will really
listen to the Word of God? I do not think there are many. That is one
reason that this hour God is permitting His Word to go to the world via
radio and why He is allowing the Word to reach groups of people that
many Christians had given up on. My friend, if the folk in churches
are not going to listen to the Word of God, He is going to go out yonder
where people *will* receive it. Daniel would not have done any good in
Jerusalem, but he was made top man in Babylon and there a pagan
king listened to him. My friend, God is going to let people hear the
gospel who are willing to listen to Him.

VISION OF THE VINE

Chapter 15 is the parable of the vine that would not bear fruit. The
vine is one of the figures of the nation Israel. In Isaiah 5 the vine set
before us is the nation Israel. We do not need to speculate about that
because Isaiah said, "For the vineyard of the LORD of hosts is the house
of Israel. . ." (Isa. 5:7).

Son of man, What is the vine tree more than any tree, or
than a branch which is among the trees of the forest?

Shall wood be taken thereof to do any work? or will men
take a pin of it to hang any vessel thereon?

Behold, it is cast into the fire for fuel; the fire devoureth
both the ends of it, and the midst of it is burned. Is it
meet for any work? [Ezek. 15:2–4].

God makes a very interesting application here. Just what is the purpose of a vine? The Lord Jesus also used the vine as a picture of believers today in John 15. He said, by the way, that Israel was no longer a vine, but "I am the true [genuine] vine . . ." (John 15:1). The Lord Jesus was not talking about salvation in that chapter. Again, I ask you: What is the purpose of a vine? It is to do one thing—bear fruit—nothing else. What God is saying here in Ezekiel is that you do not go to the furniture store and ask for a Louis XIV bedroom set made of grapevine wood! The salesman would look at you in amazement and say, "We do not have anything made of grapevine wood. It's not good for anything like that. It's just good for bearing fruit." Furthermore, God says, if a vine will not bear fruit, the only thing it is good for is burning. In John, the Lord Jesus said that if a believer does not bear fruit, you do not lose your salvation, but you are removed from the place of fruit bearing. God sets men aside in many, many ways if they do not bear fruit. The Lord Jesus said, "Herein, is my Father glorified, that ye bear much fruit . . ." (John 15:8).

The people of Israel were not bearing fruit, and God said, "There is nothing left for me to do but to burn Jerusalem." That is the reason He did it—the people were supposed to represent God, and they had failed to do it.

If you have been given great privilege as a Christian today, then you have a great responsibility. Have you ever thought of that poor fellow in Africa or China or Russia who has not had the privilege of hearing the Word of God? We who have heard His Word have a great responsibility. God wants us to be bearing fruit today.

JERUSALEM LIKENED TO AN ABANDONED BABY ADOPTED BY GOD

Chapter 16 contains yet another parable—the parable of an abandoned little orphan, a dirty and filthy little child, for whom it would seem there is nothing that can be done.

Again the word of the LORD came unto me, saying [Ezek. 16:1].

Ezekiel is not going to let us forget that he is giving us the Word of the Lord. We may not accept it, but it is still His Word.

Son of man, cause Jerusalem to know her abominations [Ezek. 16:2].

Who is the little orphan? Who is the little dirty, filthy child who has been thrown out? Who is this illegitimate child? It is the city of Jerusalem.

And say, Thus saith the Lord GOD unto Jerusalem; Thy birth and thy nativity is of the land of Canaan; thy father was an Amorite, and thy mother an Hittite [Ezek. 16:3].

This does not speak of the origin of the *nation* Israel; it is not speaking of Abraham and Sarah. The origin of the *city* of Jerusalem is in view here. The history of Jerusalem is that it was an Amorite city. We read in Genesis 15:16, "But in the fourth generation they [that is, the children of Israel] shall come hither again: for the iniquity of the Amorites is not yet full." Jerusalem was a Hittite city also. The Hittites were a great nation, and they controlled that land at one time. This is the background of Jerusalem, and it is nothing to brag about at all.

And as for thy nativity, in the day thou wast born thy navel was not cut, neither wast thou washed in water to supple thee; thou wast not salted at all, nor swaddled at all.

None eye pitied thee, to do any of these unto thee, to have compassion upon thee; but thou wast cast out in the open field, to the loathing of thy person, in the day that thou wast born [Ezek. 16:4-5].

She was an illegitimate orphan child who was just thrown out—abandoned and not cared for.

And when I passed by thee, and saw thee polluted in thine own blood, I said unto thee when thou wast in thy blood, Live; yea, I said unto thee when thou wast in thy blood, Live.

I have caused thee to multiply as the bud of the field, and thou hast increased and waxen great, and thou art come to excellent ornaments: thy breasts are fashioned, and thine hair is grown, whereas thou wast naked and bare.

Now when I passed by thee, and looked upon thee, behold, thy time was the time of love; and I spread my skirt over thee, and covered thy nakedness: yea, I sware unto thee, and entered into a covenant with thee, saith the Lord God, and thou becamest mine [Ezek. 16:6–8].

God says to Jerusalem, "I adopted you and made you My child."

Then washed I thee with water; yea, I throughly washed away thy blood from thee, and I anointed thee with oil.

I clothed thee also with broidered work, and shod thee with badgers' skin, and I girded thee about with fine linen, and I covered thee with silk.

I decked thee also with ornaments, and I put bracelets upon thy hands, and a chain on thy neck [Ezek. 16:9–11].

He says, "This is what I did for Jerusalem."

I think the application to our lives is quite obvious: you and I have a pretty bad background. Adam and Eve became sinners, and you and I were born in iniquity. David said, ". . . in sin did my mother conceive me" (Ps. 51:5), and David is no different from you and me. What do you have to boast about? Even if your ancestors *did* come over on the Mayflower, they were just a bunch of sinners saved by the grace of

God. That is our origin, our background—we were dead in trespasses and sin.

What did God do for Jerusalem? God said to her, "Live" (v. 6). To us He has said, ". . . Ye must be born again" (John 3:7). He has made a covenant that if you will trust Christ, He will save you. "For God so loved the world, that he gave his only begotten Son, that whosoever believeth in him should not perish, but have everlasting life" (John 3:16). The Lord took that little illegitimate child, dirty and filthy in its own blood, and He said, "Then washed I thee with water." Likewise, we can know the washing of regeneration and the renewing of the Holy Spirit. "I throughly washed away the blood from thee"—the Lord Jesus bore my guilt on the Cross; there is no blood guilt on a child of God today. "And I anointed thee with oil"—He anoints the child of God today with the oil of the Holy Spirit. "I girded thee about with fine linen"—we can be covered with the righteousness of Christ in order that we might stand in the presence of God.

What happened to this city? God says that when she became grown, a beautiful young lady, she played the harlot. She went over into idolatry and turned her back on Him. God have mercy on the Christian who will sell himself to the world for a bowl of pottage. Yes, Esau *did* sell out cheap, but many Christians also sell out cheap to the world today. The Devil could buy a lot of us, my friend. We so easily find ourselves going off again and again away from God and away from fellowship with Him. Oh, to be true to God in this hour in which we live!

> **When I shall bring again their captivity, the captivity of Sodom and her daughters, and the captivity of Samaria and her daughters, then will I bring again the captivity of thy captives in the midst of them:**

> **That thou mayest bear thine own shame and mayest be confounded in all that thou hast done, in that thou art a comfort unto them.**

> **When thy sisters, Sodom and her daughters, shall return to their former estate, and Samaria and her daugh-**

ters shall return to their former estate, then thou and thy daughters shall return to your former estate [Ezek. 16:53–55].

Verses 53 and 55 (as well as ch. 37) have been used by several cults to teach the doctrine of restitutionalism; that is, that everybody ultimately will be saved. Again, this is a case of resting doctrine on a few isolated verses of Scripture which will result in weird and unscriptural doctrine. In these verses and in Ezekiel 37:12, where God says, "I will open your graves, and cause you to come up out of your graves," God is *not* talking about the resurrection of the wicked to eternal life. In both instances He is talking about the restoration of a city or a nation, and it has no reference to the people who lived there years ago. Here in Ezekiel 16 He is saying that the city of Sodom is to be rebuilt. Now, personally, I don't see anything there to attract anybody, but there is tremendous development today along the coast of the Dead Sea in that area. And in chapter 37 the Lord is speaking of the restoration of a nation, the nation of Israel.

Actually, in the Old Testament we do not have the divine revelation concerning the future state that we have in the New Testament. God had no plan to bring back from the dead the saints of the Old Testament and to take them out yonder to a place prepared for them. He has told us that is His plan for us, but nowhere did He tell the Old Testament saints that. He told them there was to be a heaven down here on this earth, and that is the resurrection Abraham looked for. There is to be a restoration of the nation. You cannot read what is New Testament development of this doctrine into this Old Testament passage. However, every Old Testament passage will conform also to New Testament teaching. The New Testament makes it very clear that there will be a twofold resurrection: the resurrection of the saved, and the resurrection of the lost who are *lost* when they are raised from the dead. Therefore, these verses deal only with the restoration of a nation. We must read them in their context and not draw any more from them than is there.

This chapter concludes in a most glorious way: God is going to make good His covenants with the nation Israel. The sin of these people, their rebellion, their constant departure from Him, their backsliding, will not annul, abrogate, or destroy God's covenant with them.

> **Nevertheless I will remember my covenant with thee in the days of thy youth, and I will establish unto thee an everlasting covenant.**
>
> **Then thou shalt remember thy ways, and be ashamed, when thou shalt receive thy sisters, thine elder and thy younger: and I will give them unto thee for daughters, but not by thy covenant.**
>
> **And I will establish my covenant with thee; and thou shalt know that I am the LORD:**
>
> **That thou mayest remember, and be confounded, and never open thy mouth any more because of thy shame, when I am pacified toward thee for all that thou hast done, saith the Lord GOD [Ezek. 16:60–63].**

God says that not only will He make good on the past covenants but He is also going to make a new covenant with them. Unfortunately, these passages of Scripture are not studied very much at all. When they are, they make it very clear that God still has a future purpose with the nation Israel.

CHAPTER 17

RIDDLE OF THE TWO EAGLES

And the word of the LORD came unto me, saying,

Son of man, put forth a riddle, and speak a parable unto the house of Israel [Ezek. 17:1–2].

"**P**ut forth a riddle, and speak a parable unto the house of Israel"—because they would not listen to him, Ezekiel had to come to these people in a strange and unusual way.

And say, Thus saith the Lord GOD; A great eagle with great wings, long-winged, full of feathers, which had divers colours, came unto Lebanon, and took the highest branch of the cedar:

He cropped off the top of his young twigs, and carried it into a land of traffic; he set it in a city of merchants.

He took also of the seed of the land, and planted it in a fruitful field; he placed it by great waters, and set it as a willow tree [Ezek. 17:3–5].

This great eagle is none other than Babylon and Nebuchadnezzar, the present king of Babylon. The eagle is a figure that is used as a symbol for Babylon elsewhere in Scripture. Jeremiah used it in Jeremiah 48:40 as he wrote of Nebuchadnezzar: "For thus saith the LORD; Behold, he shall fly as an eagle, and shall spread his wings over Moab." Then in Jeremiah 49:22 he wrote, "Behold, he shall come up and fly as the eagle, and spread his wings over Bozrah: and at that day shall the heart of the mighty men of Edom be as the heart of a woman in her pangs." Daniel saw the Babylonian Empire rising up out of the sea, and it was in the form of a lion with eagle's wings (Dan. 7:4). Therefore, what we have here is a picture of Nebuchadnezzar, king of Babylon, who is going to come and crop the top of the tree.

Who is the tree? It is the nation Israel and specifically, the royal house of David. Nebuchadnezzar is going to clip it off and bring it to naught. That is exactly what he did with Zedekiah.

> **There was also another great eagle with great wings and many feathers: and, behold, this vine did bend her roots toward him, and shot forth her branches toward him, that he might water it by the furrows of her plantation [Ezek. 17:7].**

The other eagle is Egypt which was still a great power at this time. Zedekiah had been put on the throne by Nebuchadnezzar, and they made a covenant together. However, Zedekiah broke that covenant and turned to Egypt. That is pictured here by the branches which lean toward Egypt. The vine is planted in the soil of Egypt, seeking to draw strength from her, but there will not be any strength because Egypt will go down. Nebuchadnezzar took Egypt and destroyed it and made it subject to himself.

Now this is the message which grows out of Ezekiel's parable:

> **Say now to the rebellious house, Know ye not what these things mean? tell them, Behold, the king of Babylon is come to Jerusalem, and hath taken the king thereof, and the princes thereof, and led them with him to Babylon.**

> **And hath taken of the king's seed, and made a covenant with him, and hath taken an oath of him: he hath also taken the mighty of the land:**

> **That the kingdom might be base, that it might not lift itself up, but that by keeping of his covenant it might stand.**

> **But he rebelled against him in sending his ambassadors into Egypt, that they might give him horses and much**

> **people. Shall he prosper? shall he escape that doeth such things? or shall he break the covenant, and be delivered? [Ezek. 17:12–15].**

The interesting thing is that Nebuchadnezzar kept his side of the covenant. God's people broke the covenant, but the pagan nation kept their side of it. What a picture! In some churches you will find people still carrying their Bibles, but their hearts are far from God and you cannot believe what they say. On the other hand, there are businessmen who, although they are unsaved, are men of integrity.

Nebuchadnezzar is going to come and destroy Zedekiah:

> **Seeing he despised the oath by breaking the covenant, when, lo, he had given his hand, and hath done all these things, he shall not escape [Ezek. 17:18].**

God says, "I intend that Zedekiah be judged for this." My friend, I sure would hate to be some Christians who are someday going to be taken to the woodshed for the lives they have lived down here. God will certainly judge.

> **And all the trees of the field shall know that I the LORD have brought down the high tree, have exalted the low tree, have dried up the green tree, and have made the dry tree to flourish: I the LORD have spoken and have done it [Ezek. 17:24].**

Sometimes God allows a godless nation to harass and actually destroy a people who claim to be God's people but have departed from Him. There has been a great breakdown in morals in America, and apostasy is in earnest. We have not had much peace in this world, either internally or externally. There is trouble everywhere. God says that we will not get by with our sin—there will be a judgment.

CHAPTERS 18 AND 19

THEME: Jerusalem an example of "the wages of sin is death"; elegy of Jehovah over the princes of Israel

In chapter 18 God will show that in His judgment He deals specifically and individually with each person.

The word of the Lord came unto me again, saying [Ezek. 18:1].

Again, it is clear that Ezekiel is not giving his own opinion. This is God's Word.

What mean ye, that ye use this proverb concerning the land of Israel, saying, The fathers have eaten sour grapes, and the children's teeth are set on edge? [Ezek. 18:2].

The children of Israel had a proverb they used, and it is mentioned twice by Jeremiah. In Jeremiah 31:29 we read, "In those days they shall say no more, The fathers have eaten a sour grape, and the children's teeth are set on edge." And then in Lamentations 5:7 we find, "Our fathers have sinned, and are not; and we have borne their iniquities." I believe the people had built this proverb upon a passage back in Exodus: "Thou shalt not bow down thyself to them, nor serve them: for I the Lord thy God am a jealous God, visiting the iniquity of the fathers upon the children unto the third and fourth generation of them that hate me" (Exod. 20:5). The problem is that the proverb they drew from this verse is incorrect. That is the danger in lifting out one verse of Scripture without considering its context. This is a false proverb: The fathers ate the grapes, and the children paid the penalty. That is true to a certain extent, but God judges the individual, father or son, according to his conduct. This is not a judgment for eternal life, but a judgment in this life according as a man obeys or disobeys Him.

**As I live, saith the Lord God, ye shall not have occasion
any more to use this proverb in Israel [Ezek. 18:3].**

The word *live*, or some form of it occurs thirteen times in this chapter,
and the word *die* occurs fourteen times. We have life and death presented here, but it is not eternal life or eternal death that God is talking
about. God is speaking of the way in which He judges individuals in
this life. We need to look at this entire chapter from that viewpoint.

**Behold, all souls are mine; as the soul of the father, so
also the soul of the son is mine: the soul that sinneth, it
shall die [Ezek. 18:4].**

God says here that all souls belong to Him. If the sins of the fathers
come upon the children, it is because the children have followed the
wickedness of their fathers. Every man shall be put to death for his
own sin. We read in Deuteronomy 24:16, "The fathers shall not be put
to death for the children, neither shall the children be put to death for
the fathers: every man shall be put to death for his own sin."
    "The soul that sinneth, it shall die"—God will judge each individ-
ual.

**But if a man be just, and do that which is lawful and
right,**

**And hath not eaten upon the mountains, neither hath
lifted up his eyes to the idols of the house of Israel, neither hath defiled his neighbour's wife, neither hath
come near to a menstruous woman,**

**And hath not oppressed any, but hath restored to the
debtor his pledge, hath spoiled none by violence, hath
given his bread to the hungry, and hath covered the naked with a garment;**

**He that hath not given forth upon usury, neither hath
taken any increase, that hath withdrawn his hand for**

> iniquity, hath executed true judgment between man and
> man,
>
> Hath walked in my statutes, and hath kept my judg-
> ments, to deal truly; he is just, he shall surely live, saith
> the Lord God [Ezek. 18:5-9].

"Hath not eaten upon the mountains"—he has not engaged in idolatry. This man is a just man who has walked in God's statutes and kept
His ordinances. "He shall surely live, saith the Lord God." He is talking about this life, not eternal life. God will bless him in this life—
this is the blessing of the Old Testament.

> If he beget a son that is a robber, a shedder of blood, and
> that doeth the like to any one of these things [Ezek.
> 18:10].

However, the just man may have an ungodly son.

> Hath given forth upon usury, and hath taken increase:
> shall he then live? he shall not live: he hath done all
> these abominations; he shall surely die; his blood shall
> be upon him [Ezek. 18:13].

God will judge that son—not the father.

> Now, lo, if he beget a son, that seeth all his father's sins
> which he hath done, and considereth, and doeth not
> such like [Ezek. 18:14].

On the other hand, a son may decide not to follow in the footsteps of
his wicked father. There were several instances of this in the history of
Israel. Old Ahaz was a wicked king, but his son Hezekiah led in a
revival. Josiah was a wonderful man, and he had a very wicked father.

> That hath taken off his hand from the poor, that hath not
> received usury nor increase, hath executed my judg-

> ments, hath walked in my statutes; he shall not die for
> the iniquity of his father, he shall surely live.
>
> As for his father, because he cruelly oppressed, spoiled
> his brother by violence, and did that which is not good
> among his people, lo, even he shall die in his iniquity
> [Ezek. 18:17–18].

God is saying that each man is judged in this life for the way he lives
his life. Remember that He is not speaking of eternal life but about
judgment here and now. He wants Israel to know this is the basis on
which He intends to judge them.

> The soul that sinneth, it shall die. The son shall not bear
> the iniquity of the father, neither shall the father bear the
> iniquity of the son: the righteousness of the righteous
> shall be upon him, and the wickedness of the wicked
> shall be upon him [Ezek. 18:20].

"The soul that sinneth, it shall die." We have this twice in this
chapter—here and in verse 4.

> Cast away from you all your transgressions, whereby ye
> have transgressed; and make you a new heart and a new
> spirit: for why will ye die, O house of Israel? [Ezek.
> 18:31].

The teaching of this chapter answers the new psychology we have
today. Psychology argues that the reason a person is a brat or an odd-
ball is because his mother didn't treat him right but neglected him
and didn't love him. My friend, you stand alone. You are a sinner
because you are a sinner yourself. There's an old bromide that is rather
crude, but it certainly expresses it well: Every tub must sit on its own
bottom. Every individual will stand before God, and he won't be able
to blame his papa and mama at that time. Ezekiel makes it very clear

that the Israelite will be judged in this life on the basis of the life he lived, whether he was a believer or not.

> **For I have no pleasure in the death of him that dieth, saith the Lord GOD: wherefore turn yourselves, and live ye [Ezek. 18:32].**

Again, this refers to physical death. God does not take any delight today in seeing anyone die. That is something that is foreign to Him; He didn't intend death for mankind. Remember that the Lord Jesus *wept* at the tomb of Lazarus, even though He was going to bring him back into this life. By man came death, not through the working of God, but because of man's sin.

ELEGY OF JEHOVAH OVER
THE PRINCES OF ISRAEL

In chapter 19 we have two lamentations: the lamentations over the princes of Israel (vv. 1–9), and the lamentation over the land of Judah, the southern kingdom of Israel (vv. 10–14).

> **Moreover take thou up a lamentation for the princes of Israel,**
>
> **And say, What is thy mother? A lioness: she lay down among lions, she nourished her whelps among young lions.**
>
> **And she brought up one of her whelps: it became a young lion, and it learned to catch the prey; it devoured men [Ezek. 19:1–3].**

This is not the lamentation of Ezekiel, as some Bible commentators have attempted to say. This is the lamentation of the Lord, actually the lamentation of the same One who later wept over Jerusalem (Matt. 23:37–39). He is the One who is here weeping over the princes of Judah. The princes were a group of people in that land who had very few who were concerned about them. But God was concerned. Who shed tears over them? God did.

By the way, who is concerned about you today? I suspect there are very few. Are the people where you work really concerned about you? Are the people in your church really concerned about you? Is your family concerned? A successful businessman once told me, "I honestly wonder who really cares about me today. Everybody, including my family, is only interested in what they can get out of me." How sad that is! But God is concerned about you, and He is concerned about me. That's quite comforting in this tremendous universe in which I live. I could get lost in it, I am so small. But He has His eye out and has a concern for each one of us.

The princes of Judah were people for whom not too many in that day wanted to shed tears. They were Jehoahaz and Jehoiachin, two kings who were about as sorry as they come. God alone is concerned over them.

When He begins to speak of the "lion," He is speaking of the lion of Judah. "Judah is a lion's whelps . . ."—that is the way Judah was marked out by Jacob in Genesis 49:9 as he gave his prophecies concerning each of his twelve sons. In Numbers 23:24 we read, "Behold, the people shall rise up as a great lion, and lift up himself as a young lion. . . ." The Lord Jesus is called the Lion of the tribe of Juda in Revelation 5:5: "And one of the elders saith unto me, Weep not: behold, the Lion of the tribe of Juda, the Root of David, hath prevailed to open the book, and to loose the seven seals thereof."

Thy mother is like a vine in thy blood, planted by the waters: she was fruitful and full of branches by reason of many waters.

And she had strong rods for the sceptres of them that bare rule, and her stature was exalted among the thick branches, and she appeared in her height with the multitude of her branches.

But she was plucked up in fury, she was cast down to the ground, and the east wind dried up her fruit: her strong rods were broken and withered; the fire consumed them [Ezek. 19:10–12].

This now is the lamentation over the land of Judah. These people came into that land, and God blessed them. They were like a vine planted in the land. Now He has plucked up the vine, and they are carried away into captivity. This is a sad song depicting the sordid history of the nation.

CHAPTER 20

THEME: Review of Israel's long history of sins; future judgment and restoration

Chapters 20—24 contain the final predictions concerning the judgment of Jerusalem. There are two things to which I would like to call your attention in this section. First, notice how long and drawn out is God's message to these people. Right down to the very day that Nebuchadnezzar besieged the city, God was willing to spare them. God would have removed Nebuchadnezzar from the city as He had done previously to the Assyrians and would not have permitted him to destroy it. However, the people did not turn to God, and the judgment came. Right down to the last moment there was mercy extended to them. Second, the very day that the siege of Jerusalem began, the wife of Ezekiel died, and God told him not to mourn or weep for her at all. I consider this man Ezekiel a sharp contrast to the prophet Jeremiah. Jeremiah had a woman's heart, and he wept; the message he gave broke his own heart. Because He wept, the Lord Jesus was compared to Jeremiah. I'll be honest with you though; Ezekiel is almost like an actor playing a part. He goes through his part, but he is not moved by it. He seems to be pretty hardboiled all the way through. Ezekiel was simply a mouthpiece for God.

REVIEW OF ISRAEL'S LONG HISTORY OF SINS; FUTURE JUDGMENT AND RESTORATION

In chapter 20 we have a retrospect of the nation's sins. Again, it is Ezekiel giving not his word, but God's Word. He was very much like a Western Union boy who brings you a message. It may be a message of joy, it may be a message of sorrow, but the Western Union boy just delivers the message—you are the one who is moved by it.

> **And it came to pass in the seventh year, in the fifth month, the tenth day of the month, that certain of the**

elders of Israel came to inquire of the LORD, and sat before me [Ezek. 20:1].

More and more they are beginning to turn to this man Ezekiel—they
come now to get a word. This occurred in approximately 590 B.C. The
destruction of Jerusalem took place shortly after, somewhere around
588–586 B.C. I do not think we can be dogmatic about these dates.

Then came the word of the LORD unto me, saying [Ezek.
20:2].

He is not giving his word, he is giving God's Word.

Son of man, speak unto the elders of Israel, and say unto
them, Thus saith the Lord GOD; Are ye come to inquire
of me? As I live, saith the Lord GOD, I will not be inquired of by you.

Wilt thou judge them, son of man, wilt thou judge them?
cause them to know the abominations of their fathers
[Ezek. 20:3–4].

These people are coming to complain and to criticize God. They say
He is unfair to judge them and unfair to destroy Jerusalem. It is beginning to penetrate their thinking that it is really going to happen.

Ezekiel is going to go over this ground again with them because
God does not mind stating His charge or reviewing His reasons for the
judgment He is to bring.

And say unto them, Thus saith the Lord GOD; In the day
when I chose Israel, and lifted up mine hand unto the
seed of the house of Jacob, and made myself known unto
them in the land of Egypt, when I lifted up mine hand
unto them, saying, I am the LORD your God [Ezek. 20:5].

God goes back to the very beginning when He called these people out
of the land of Egypt, delivered them out of their slavery there, and
brought them into the wilderness.

> But the house of Israel rebelled against me in the wilderness: they walked not in my statutes, and they despised my judgments, which if a man do, he shall even live in them; and my sabbaths they greatly polluted: then I said, I would pour out my fury upon them in the wilderness, to consume them [Ezek. 20:13].

The generation that went into the wilderness rebelled against God, and He let them die in the wilderness.

> Notwithstanding the children rebelled against me: they walked not in my statutes, neither kept my judgments to do them, which if a man do, he shall even live in them; they polluted my sabbaths: then I said, I would pour out my fury upon them, to accomplish my anger against them in the wilderness.
>
> Nevertheless I withdrew mine hand, and wrought for my name's sake, that it should not be polluted in the sight of the heathen, in whose sight I brought them forth [Ezek. 20:21–22].

The next generation was rebellious also.

> Wherefore I gave them also statutes that were not good, and judgments whereby they should not live;
>
> And I polluted them in their own gifts, in that they caused to pass through the fire all that openeth the womb, that I might make them desolate, to the end that they might know that I am the LORD [Ezek. 20:25–26].

This is a strange passage of Scripture, and there is a difference of opinion among commentators as to what it means. I feel that the thought here is the same thought Paul had in 2 Corinthians 2:15–16— "For we are unto God as a sweet savour of Christ, in them that are saved, and in them that perish: To the one we are the savour of death unto death; and to the other the savour of life unto life. . . ." When God gave these people His Word and they rejected it, He gave them over to their own way. The very law that was good became bad because it condemned them and judged them. The same thing is true of the gospel today. If you listen to the gospel and reject it, it would actually be better if you had never heard it. If you reject it, the gospel becomes a savor of death unto you. You can never go before God and say that you had not heard it.

Considering this tremendous condemnation, you would think God was through with these people. But tucked in here and there throughout the Book of Ezekiel we find marvelous, wonderful passages of promise. At the darkest time in their history, the light of prophecy shone the brightest.

> **As I live, saith the Lord God, surely with a mighty hand, and with a stretched out arm, and with fury poured out, will I rule over you:**
>
> **And I will bring you out from the people, and will gather you out of the countries wherein ye are scattered, with a mighty hand, and with a stretched out arm, and with fury poured out [Ezek. 20:33–34].**

God tells them that He intends to bring them back into the land. God's purpose with Israel will yet be fulfilled. He will someday be declared right by those who had said He was not right.

> **Moreover the word of the Lord came unto me, saying,**
>
> **Son of man, set thy face toward the south, and drop thy word toward the south, and prophesy against the forest of the south field;**
>
> **And say to the forest of the south, Hear the word of the Lord; Thus saith the Lord God; Behold, I will kindle a fire in thee, and it shall devour every green tree in thee, and every dry tree: the flaming flame shall not be**

**quenched, and all faces from the south to the north shall
be burned therein [Ezek. 20:45–47].**

"Prophesy against the forest of the south field"—some commentators
feel this refers to Judah, and others think it means the Negeb. At least,
it is south. If you were to see the Negeb, you would wonder what happened to the forest. Well, my friend, God judged it; He said He would
remove it. That land was once the land of milk and honey, but you
cannot come to that conclusion when you look at it today. Not only is
it not the land of milk and honey, they do not even have enough water
there.

This is a remarkable prophecy. God is not through with these people or with that land.

CHAPTER 21

THEME: Babylon removes last Davidic king until Messiah comes

It is important to study the Book of Ezekiel because it is so often neglected and its message is very pertinent for this hour in which we are living today. Although the words of Ezekiel were spoken many years ago, it was the Word of God as he has almost monotonously repeated: "The word of the Lord came unto me, saying." Since it is the Word of God, it has an application for us in this day and in this nation. The liberal argues that, like the Book of Revelation, the Book of Ezekiel cannot be understood and does not have a message for us. Ezekiel's visions are tremendous, and I do not propose to have the final word on their interpretation. I just stand in awe and wonder. But in this section of the book we are down to the nitty-gritty where the rubber meets the road, and I am sincere when I say that Ezekiel is not difficult to understand and he is very practical for us.

Chapter 21 is one of the most important chapters in the Book of Ezekiel as it makes it very clear that the king of Babylon is going to remove the last king of the Davidic line until Messiah comes.

And the word of the Lord came unto me, saying [Ezek. 21:1].

Ezekiel will repeat this three times in this chapter. There is only one alternative for you: either you agree that the Lord said this, or you take the position that Ezekiel is lying. I believe that the Lord said this to him and that Ezekiel is not giving his viewpoint. I do not think that Ezekiel's feelings entered into his message very much. Jeremiah was overwhelmed by his feelings; they entered into every word he spoke. I do not think that is true of Ezekiel. In the beginning of his ministry when God gave Ezekiel his commission, He told him that he was going to speak to a rebellious and hardheaded people. God also said at that time He would make Ezekiel's head harder than theirs. I think maybe a little of that hardness got down to his heart, and so he could really lay it on the line to these people. You actually love the man for this, for, if his feelings had entered into it, this man would have been crushed by the message that he had to give.

> **Son of man, set thy face toward Jerusalem, and drop thy word toward the holy places, and prophesy against the land of Israel,**
>
> **And say to the land of Israel, Thus saith the LORD; Behold, I am against thee, and will draw forth my sword out of his sheath, and will cut off from thee the righteous and the wicked [Ezek. 21:2–3].**

Judgment is impending and apparently now is inevitable. Up to this point, the mercy of God has been extended, but now judgment is coming and there is no alternative.

"Thus saith the LORD; Behold, I am against thee." This is the first time He has said this about His city of Jerusalem.

"And will cut off from thee the righteous and the wicked." This sounds strange, does it not? Who are the righteous? The ones who say they are righteous? In our day they are the ones who are church members but are not saved at all, the ones who go through the ritual, who are religious. A great many people have the band-aid of religion over the sore of sin. They need to pull that old band-aid off and get that sore lanced before it destroys them. It's a cancerous sore, and you simply do not cure cancer by putting a band-aid over it. Neither do you cure sin by becoming religious. God said, "I'm cutting it off now; I'm moving in with the sword, and I intend to destroy the city."

> **Seeing then that I will cut off from thee the righteous and the wicked, therefore shall my sword go forth out of his sheath against all flesh from the south to the north [Ezek. 21:4].**

He is going to draw out the sword from its sheath—all the way from the south to the north.

That all flesh may know that I the LORD have drawn forth my sword out of his sheath: it shall not return any more [Ezek. 21:5].

"It shall not return any more"—the time for judgment has come.

Sigh therefore, thou son of man, with the breaking of thy loins; and with bitterness sigh before their eyes.

And it shall be, when they say unto thee, Wherefore sighest thou? that thou shalt answer, For the tidings; because it cometh: and every heart shall melt, and all hands shall be feeble, and every spirit shall faint, and all knees shall be weak as water: behold, it cometh, and shall be brought to pass, saith the Lord GOD [Ezek. 21:6–7].

God asks Ezekiel to do something here, and I am not prepared to say whether Ezekiel's feelings are in it or not. He didn't do it naturally— God told him to do it—so I would say that he is acting the part. However, in doing so, he is revealing the heart of God.

The people have complained about Ezekiel's giving parables to them. In Ezekiel 20:49 we read, "Then said I, Ah, Lord GOD! they say of me, Doth he not speak parables?" In effect, they were saying, "We don't get his message." They didn't *want* to get it; they didn't like to be told that things were wrong. We sometimes think that the parables of the Lord Jesus are obtuse and difficult to understand. They are not, if you *want* to understand them. The religious rulers in His day understood what He was saying—that is the reason they hated Him. They understood He was speaking judgment against them.

Again the word of the LORD came unto me, saying [Ezek. 21:8].

Just in case you didn't get the message, Ezekiel repeats it again.

> **Son of man, prophesy, and say, Thus saith the LORD; Say, A sword, a sword is sharpened, and also furbished:**

> **It is sharpened to make a sore slaughter; it is furbished that it may glitter: should we then make mirth? it contemneth the rod of my son, as every tree [Ezek. 21:9–10].**

God is going to judge the city. This is a frightful and fearful word which comes from the lips of God, the One who had yearned over Jerusalem. The Lord Jesus, too, *wept* over Jerusalem because He loved the city: "O Jerusalem, Jerusalem, thou that killest the prophets, and stonest them which are sent unto thee, how often would I have gathered thy children together, even as a hen gathereth her chickens under her wings, and ye would not! Behold, your house is left unto you desolate" (Matt. 23:37–38). If you want to know how terrible that judgment was, read what happened when Titus the Roman came in A.D. 70 and leveled that city—just as Nebuchadnezzar is about to do in Ezekiel's time.

God makes it clear what He is going to do, and the message is not a brand new one by any means. In the Book of Isaiah we find: "For by fire and by his sword will the LORD plead with all flesh: and the slain of the LORD shall be many" (Isa. 66:16). And again we read, "Fear, and the pit, and the snare, are upon thee, O inhabitant of the earth" (Isa. 24:17). Ezekiel is to sigh because of the judgment that is coming. The Lord Jesus said of the day that is still coming, "Men's hearts failing them for fear, and for looking after those things which are coming on the earth: for the powers of heaven shall be shaken" (Luke 21:26). Ezekiel is to sigh and weep because God has now drawn the sword of judgment. Judgment lies ahead in our day, my friend. That is not a popular message, just as it was not in Ezekiel's day.

> **The word of the LORD came unto me again, saying [Ezek. 21:18].**

Believe me, he will not let us forget this!

> Also, thou son of man, appoint thee two ways, that the
> sword of the king of Babylon may come: both twain
> shall come forth out of one land: and choose thou a
> place, choose it at the head of the way to the city [Ezek.
> 21:19].

In other words, Nebuchadnezzar wanted to decide which way he was
going to come to Jerusalem. Now, do you think he's going to turn to
the Lord? No, he is pagan. He is going to use divination and necro-
mancy:

> For the king of Babylon stood at the parting of the way,
> at the head of the two ways, to use divination: he made
> his arrows bright, he consulted with images, he looked
> in the liver [Ezek. 21:21].

These are methods which were used in that day and are actually used
today also.

"He made his arrows bright" would be better translated as, "he
shook his arrows to and fro." This was sort of like rolling dice or looking at tea leaves. He dropped his arrows down to see which direction
they pointed to determine which direction he should take to Jerusalem. Nebuchadnezzar was entirely a pagan and heathen king. God,
however, will overrule his actions—that is important to remember.

> And thou, profane wicked prince of Israel, whose day is
> come, when iniquity shall have an end [Ezek. 21:25].

"Thou, profane wicked prince of Israel"—he is speaking of Zedekiah.
"Whose day is come, when iniquity shall have an end"—the time for
judgment has come; this is the end time.

Scripture has a great deal to say about the end of this age. The
correct translation of Ezekiel's phrase would be, "in the time of the
iniquity of the end." Daniel also used this expression, ". . . the time of

the end . . ." (Dan. 11:35). The disciples asked the Lord Jesus, ". . . Tell us, when shall these things be? and what shall be the sign of thy coming, and of the end of the world?" (Matt. 24:3), and the Lord answered that question for them. Paul also spoke of it a great deal in 2 Thessalonians. This man, Zedekiah, then is a picture of that future wicked prince, the false messiah, the Antichrist, who is coming at the time of the end.

> **Thus saith the Lord GOD; Remove the diadem, and take off the crown: this shall not be the same: exalt him that is low, and abase him that is high [Ezek. 21:26].**

Zedekiah is to be brought low, and there will not be another king to sit upon the throne of David "until Shiloh come," until the Messiah comes.

> **I will overturn, overturn, overturn, it: and it shall be no more, until he come whose right it is; and I will give it him [Ezek. 21:27].**

This is a remarkable prophecy. "Until he come whose right it is; and I will give it him," that is, the Lord Jesus. From Zedekiah down to the Lord Jesus there has been no one in the line of David who ever sat on that throne. Ezekiel is saying that no one would ever be able to do so. The Lord Jesus is the only One who will. Right now He is sitting at God's right hand, waiting until His enemies are made His footstool when He comes to this earth to rule.

This remarkable prophecy began back in Genesis 49:10, when Jacob was giving the prophecies concerning his twelve sons who became the twelve tribes of Israel. He said there: "The sceptre shall not depart from Judah, nor a lawgiver from between his feet, until Shiloh come; and unto him shall the gathering of the people be." "The sceptre" means the king. The Hebrew word for "until He come" is very similar to the word, *Shiloh*. It speaks of the Lord Jesus—this is the way He was introduced in Scripture. This is the reason that John the Baptist said, ". . . Repent ye: for the kingdom of heaven is at hand" (Matt.

3:2). Why? Because it was "at hand" in the Person of the One who had come, the One of whom all the prophets had spoken.

> **Whiles they see vanity unto thee, whiles they divine a lie unto thee, to bring thee upon the necks of them that are slain, of the wicked, whose day is come, when their iniquity shall have an end [Ezek. 21:29].**

Ezekiel is speaking of the judgment of the Ammonites, but we also have again the expression, "when their iniquity shall have an end," suggesting the end of this age. In 2 Thessalonians 2:8 Paul writes: "And then shall that Wicked be revealed, whom the Lord shall consume with the spirit of his mouth, and shall destroy with the brightness of his coming." The Lord Jesus Christ will put down this enemy in the last days.

> **And I will pour out mine indignation upon thee, I will blow against thee in the fire of my wrath, and deliver thee into the hand of brutish men, and skilful to destroy.**

> **Thou shalt be for fuel to the fire; thy blood shall be in the midst of the land; thou shalt be no more remembered: for I the LORD have spoken it [Ezek. 21:31–32].**

Ezekiel's generation was going to go into captivity—that would be the end as far as they were concerned. It would be their children who would return back to the land of Israel.

CHAPTERS 22—24

THEME: Review of Jerusalem's abominations; the parable of two sisters; the parable of the boiling pot

We continue in this section which contains the last prophecies concerning the judgment that was coming upon the nation Israel (chs. 20—24). In the beginning, Ezekiel's messages were directed to the first two delegations which had gone into captivity. They were holding on to the belief that God would never destroy the temple; it was His sanctuary, and His glory had been there.

They believed that God would not allow Nebuchadnezzar to touch it. The false prophets encouraged the captives in their unbelief, making them think it was not necessary for them to come back to God, or to give up their idolatry and other evil ways.

There is something very subtle that happens often in our day which I think we need to be very careful about. A great many men are eulogized today even before they die, but particularly at their funerals; though they were godless blasphemers, some preacher tries to push them right into heaven with his words of praise. Unless we have God's mind on the matter, we need to be very careful what we say about folk. Otherwise, an unbeliever may measure his goodness by the life of someone who is praised (he knows how great a sinner that man was!), and may be led to believe that he does not need the Savior. It is tragic today that gospel messages are frequently given to a crowd of saints, but not given at a time and place the worldly and unsaved man is present. Too often, the preacher trims his message to please the crowd—that is what the false prophets of Ezekiel's day did.

Ezekiel has really been laying it on the line in these final prophecies. In chapter 20 he gave a prophecy concerning the Negeb, the southern part of Israel around Beersheba. In that prophecy God said, "I'll kindle a fire in thee." I have been through that area, and it is as baldheaded as a doorknob; there is no vegetation of any size whatsoever. I never saw a tree any larger than my arm in the entire place.

There used to be a forest there, but God judged it, and He did a pretty good job of it. Then in chapter 21, there was the remarkable prophecy that there would be no one to sit on David's throne until the Lord Jesus came. That is what the angel was talking about when he said to Mary, "I am going to give to Him the throne of His father David." You see, even at Christmastime it's nice to have Ezekiel around to add to our understanding. The background the prophets give us is so needful today.

REVIEW OF THE ABOMINATIONS OF JERUSALEM

Chapter 22 lists the abominations of the city of Jerusalem.

Moreover the word of the LORD came unto me, saying,

Now, thou son of man, wilt thou judge, wilt thou judge the bloody city? yea, thou shalt shew her all her abominations [Ezek. 22:1–2].

"The bloody city"—this is what Ezekiel calls Jerusalem. Isaiah said the same thing in Isaiah 1:21, "How is the faithful city become an harlot! it was full of judgment; righteousness lodged in it; but now murderers." The Lord Jesus wept over the city and said, "O Jerusalem, Jerusalem, which killest the prophets, and stonest them that are sent unto thee . . ." (Luke 13:34). After all, didn't they slay Him also? They turned Him over to the Romans who did the killing job. It was Stephen who said to the Jews, "Which of the prophets have not your fathers persecuted? and they have slain them which shewed before of the coming of the Just One; of whom ye have been now the betrayers and murderers" (Acts 7:52). At the death of Christ, the crowd cried out to Pilate, ". . . His blood be on us, and on our children" (Matt. 27:25).

The leaders of Israel were involved in apostasy and gross sins:

There is a conspiracy of her prophets in the midst thereof, like a roaring lion ravening the prey; they have devoured souls; they have taken the treasure and pre-

> cious things; they have made her many widows in the
> midst thereof [Ezek. 22:25].

Her false prophets were saying, "Everything is fine. We're getting
along nicely."

> Her priests have violated my law, and have profaned
> mine holy things: they have put no difference between
> the holy and profane, neither have they shewed differ-
> ence between the unclean and the clean, and have hid
> their eyes from my sabbaths, and I am profaned among
> them [Ezek. 22:26].

Her priests blatantly violated the law of God.

> Her princes in the midst thereof are like wolves raven-
> ing the prey, to shed blood, and to destroy souls, to get
> dishonest gain [Ezek. 22:27].

Her princes were "like wolves ravening the prey." Paul has warned the
church about wolves in sheep's clothing (see Acts 20:29), and we do
have them in the church today.

Why was Jerusalem called a bloody city? Because of the prophets,
the priests, and the princes.

> And I sought for a man among them, that should make
> up the hedge, and stand in the gap before me for the
> land, that I should not destroy it: but I found none.
>
> Therefore have I poured out mine indignation upon
> them; I have consumed them with the fire of my wrath:
> their own way have I recompensed upon their heads,
> saith the Lord GOD [Ezek. 22:30–31].

There was not a man to be found in the land who could stand in the
gap. I thank God He did find a Man to stand between my sin and a

holy God. That Man is the Lord Jesus Christ, and God sees those who belong to Him in Christ. I am thankful for the Man who stands in the gap today!

PARABLE OF TWO SISTERS

Once again, in chapter 23, Ezekiel goes way out on a limb, he goes way out into left field, and he tells the people another strange parable. It is the parable of two sisters: one was named Aholah, and the other was Aholibah. I think that when he began to give this parable, the people actually smiled and said, "Where in the world is this fellow going with a story like that?"

> The word of the LORD came again unto me, saying [Ezek. 23:1].

Ezekiel didn't make this story up—God gave him this message.

> Son of man, there were two women, the daughters of one mother:

> And they committed whoredoms in Egypt; they committed whoredoms in their youth: there were their breasts pressed, and there they bruised the teats of their virginity [Ezek. 23:2–3].

The two sisters were no longer virgins but had become harlots. What in the world is Ezekiel talking about?

> And the names of them were Aholah the elder, and Aholibah her sister: and they were mine, and they bare sons and daughters. Thus were their names; Samaria is Aholah, and Jerusalem Aholibah [Ezek. 23:4].

"Samaria is Aholah"—that is, the northern kingdom of Israel is Aholah. "And Jerusalem Aholibah"—Jerusalem and Judah in the south is Aholibah.

The meaning of *Aholibah* (Jerusalem and Judah) is, "My tent is in her." Who is saying this? God is saying, "My tent is in her." In other words, in the southern kingdom, in Jerusalem, was the wonderful temple of Solomon. It was patterned after the tabernacle in the wilderness, and it was the place where the people approached God. That was wonderful.

Aholah means "her own tent." The northern kingdom rebelled and separated from the southern part of Israel. Old King Jeroboam put up two golden calves, one in Bethel and one in Samaria, and tried to keep his people from going south to worship in Jerusalem.

It was very easy for the prophets and the people of the southern kingdom to say that God will judge those golden calves in the north—and He surely did. However, He is going to judge the southern kingdom also, because they were going through the ritual of a dead religion; they thought they were right with God, but they actually were living in sin.

One of the things that is cutting the nerve of the spiritual life even of fundamental Christians and fundamental churches today is the lives of some church members. Of course you are saved by grace—that is the only way you and I can ever be saved. If God is not going to save by grace, then I couldn't possibly be saved, but that does not mean that I am not to live for Him. That doesn't mean that He will not judge you and me. That does not mean that our lives cannot kill the spiritual life in a church.

Ezekiel attracted a little attention with his story about these two girls, Aholah and Aholibah. This incident reminds me of the whimsical story which comes out of my southland about a poor tenant farmer who had a little donkey. He hitched the donkey up to a wagon in which one line was leather and the other was a cotton rope. One day he was going to give a friend a ride into town. The friend got into the wagon, but the farmer went and got a two-by-four out of the wagon, took it up to the front, and hit his donkey on the head! The friend was thunderstruck; he couldn't believe what he saw. "Why in the world did you do that?" he asked. "Well," the farmer said. "I always have to get his attention before I start." Ezekiel was dealing with a lot of hard-headed people, and he tells this parable to get their attention. Sometimes preachers are criticized for using sensational subjects for their messages, but I have great sympathy for them. How else are you going to get people to listen today? Ezekiel used some unusual methods.

She doted upon the Assyrians her neighbours, captains and rulers clothed most gorgeously, horsemen riding upon horses, all of them desirable young men [Ezek. 23:12].

This refers to a historical event which took place when Old King Ahaz was on the throne in the southern kingdom. He went up to Damascus to meet Tiglath-pileser, king of Assyria, and he saw there an altar he thought was the prettiest altar he'd ever seen. So he sent Urijah the priest to get the pattern of it in order to make one just like it (2 Kings 16:10–18). He wanted to "improve the worship," you know—he went in for that type of thing. Well, God took note of that, and He judged the northern kingdom for it.

Now the Babylonian invasion of the southern kingdom is about to take place—there's no alternative in it. God is judging both the northern and the southern kingdoms because they have turned away from the living and true God; one went brazenly into idolatry, and the other pretended to worship the Lord.

My friend, it might be well for all of God's people to heed Paul's warning: "Examine yourselves, whether ye be in the faith . . ." (2 Cor. 13:5). Someone may ask, "Don't you believe in the security of the believer?" Yes, I do, but I also believe in the insecurity of make-believers. We need to examine ourselves. When you go to church do you really worship God? Do you draw close to the person of Christ? Do you really love Him? He doesn't want your service unless you do. In John 21 He asked Peter, "Lovest thou me?" When Peter could say that he did, then the Lord said, "Feed my sheep." Only then could the Lord use him.

PARABLE OF THE BOILING POT

In chapter 24 we have the parable of the boiling pot and the death of Ezekiel's wife. God will use both of these to speak to the people.

> **Again in the ninth year, in the tenth month, in the tenth day of the month, the word of the LORD came unto me, saying,**
>
> **Son of man, write thee the name of the day, even of this same day: the king of Babylon set himself against Jerusalem this same day [Ezek. 24:1-2].**

This is the first time that Ezekiel has dated his message. At this very moment Nebuchadnezzar was breaking through the wall of Jerusalem. There was no television in that day to let Ezekiel know what was happening. There was no satellite to convey this message from Jerusalem to Babylon. The only way he could get this message was by God revealing it to him. The liberal theologians have always had a problem with this verse; one of them has said, "This verse forces on us in the clearest fashion the dilemma that either Ezekiel was a deliberate deceiver, or he was possessed of some kind of second sight." He certainly was possessed of second sight—God's sight, by the way. The liberal doesn't recognize it as that, of course.

> **Wherefore thus saith the Lord GOD; Woe to the bloody city, to the pot whose scum is therein, and whose scum is not gone out of it! bring it out piece by piece; let no lot fall upon it [Ezek. 24:6].**

Again, Jerusalem is called "the bloody city." There is a pot, and there is scum in the pot. The pot is the city of Jerusalem; the citizens are in that pot. Their sin is the scum that's in the pot.

Sometimes we hear somebody say concerning another group of people, "They are the scum of the earth." Do you want to know what God says? He says your sin and my sin is the scum of the earth. Listen carefully: We are *all* in the same pot. The pot of Jerusalem is the pot of the world for you and me today. I get a little weary of all this talk about different "ethnic groups." We're all in the same pot, and we are the scum of the earth—that is, our sin is the scum of the earth. I don't know how you could say it more strongly than that.

Also the word of the LORD came unto me, saying,

Son of man, behold, I take away from thee the desire of thine eyes with a stroke: yet neither shalt thou mourn nor weep, neither shall thy tears run down [Ezek. 24:15-16].

Apparently, the prophet had married a lovely, young Israelite girl, and they loved each other. But down there in captivity, she became sick and died. I imagine it was a heartbreak to Ezekiel, but again he must act a part:

Forbear to cry, make no mourning for the dead, bind the tire of thine head upon thee, and put on thy shoes upon thy feet, and cover not thy lips, and eat not the bread of men [Ezek. 24:17].

God told him, "Don't act like you're mourning at all." And the people didn't understand it. The people came to Ezekiel and said, "What in the world does this mean? Your wife has died, and you are not mourning at all! What kind of man are you?"

All of this Ezekiel is doing to get a message through to the people. Verse 24 is the key to this entire Book of Ezekiel:

Thus Ezekiel is unto you a sign: according to all that he hath done shall ye do: and when this cometh, ye shall know that I am the Lord GOD [Ezek. 24:24].

At that very moment, Jerusalem was being destroyed, and later on word came to the captives about its destruction: "And it came to pass in the twelfth year of our captivity, in the tenth month, in the fifth day of the month, that one that had escaped out of Jerusalem came unto me, saying, The city is smitten" (Ezek. 33:21). Into the camp came these stragglers; they must have looked terrible. They said, "We've escaped from the city. The false prophets were wrong. The city is burned. The temple has been leveled, and the city is debris and ashes."

Ezekiel was right in not mourning. The reason they were not to mourn is found in verse 27:

> **In that day shall thy mouth be opened to him which is escaped, and thou shalt speak, and be no more dumb: and thou shalt be a sign unto them; and they shall know that I am the LORD [Ezek. 24:27].**

"They shall know that I am the Lord." Jerusalem was *God's* city, and the temple was *His* house. They were God's witness to the world. And when the people of Israel failed, God said, "I will destroy even My own witness on the earth. I want you to know the city is destroyed. The rest of your people are being brought into captivity. But there's no use weeping, there's no use howling to Me now. I have done this—I am responsible for it."

To each of the seven churches in the Book of Revelation, the Lord Jesus said, "You had better be careful of your witness to the world, or I will come and remove your lampstand." The lampstand of all seven of those churches has been removed, my friend. Not one of those churches remains today. This ought to be a message to us: If you are a Christian and are not going to stand for God today, He will remove your lampstand—there will be no light.

This is a strong message; it is not the lovey-dovey, sloppy stuff we hear so often. This is Ezekiel, and he is speaking for God. He has said again and again, "The word of the LORD, came unto me, saying." If you want to argue with his message, take it to the Lord, but remember He's right and we are the ones who are wrong.

CHAPTER 25

THEME: Prophecies against the nations: the Ammonites, Moab, Edom, the Philistines

This brings us to a new section (chs. 25—32) which deals with the prophecies concerning the nations around Israel. All of these nations, as far as we are concerned today, have long since disappeared from the face of the earth, and the prophecies about them have been literally fulfilled.

Up to this point, Ezekiel has been giving out prophecies concerning Jerusalem and the land of Israel because the *final* deportation of the children of Israel has not yet arrived. To the very last, the people held on to the faint hope, at the urging and encouragement of the false prophets, that God would not destroy Jerusalem and the land of Israel would remain. After all, wasn't it God's method of communication to the world? When the destruction of Jerusalem occurred, the people were startled; they were dumbfounded. I imagine the word came when the headline in the *Babylonian Bugle* read: JERUSALEM DESTROYED! And the opening line read something like this: "On this day Nebuchadnezzar with his armies entered the city of Jerusalem, having breached the wall."

Ezekiel was proved accurate in his prophecies, and from here on he will not be giving any prophecies concerning the destruction of Jerusalem because he is not writing *history;* he is writing *prophecy.* So now he turns to the surroundings nations. What will be their fate?

There is a tremendous message for us in this chapter. There lies God's city in ruins. I see standing over that city a man by the name of Jeremiah. Tears are coursing down his cheeks; he is a man with a broken heart. He is the one who mirrors the One who will be coming to earth in five hundred or so years. He, too, will sit over Jerusalem on the Mount of Olives and will weep over the city knowing that destruction is coming again because its people will have turned their backs on the living and true God.

I see another prophet. He is not weeping, and I will tell you why. At this same time his lovely wife died, and the Scriptures make it clear that he loved her. This prophet is Ezekiel, and he is told not to mourn. On the surface he is hard-boiled.

God said that He would be that way. Jeremiah and Ezekiel reveal the two sides of God in this matter. This is something we need to see today. God is tenderhearted. Like Jeremiah, the Lord Jesus Christ is merciful and kind. He was not willing that any should perish, so He died on the cross for us. But listen to Him speaking to the cities that rejected Him: "Woe unto thee, Chorazin! woe unto thee Bethsaida! for if the mighty works had been done in Tyre and Sidon, which have been done in you, they had a great while ago repented, sitting in sackcloth and ashes. But it shall be more tolerable for Tyre and Sidon at the judgment, than for you. And thou, Capernaum, which art exalted to heaven, shalt be thrust down to hell" (Luke 10:13–15). That is strong language coming from the gentle Jesus! He also said, "Woe unto you, scribes and Pharisees, hypocrites! for ye are as graves which appear not, and the men that walk over them are not aware of them" (Luke 11:44). The Lord denounced them in such a way that it makes your hair curl! There are two sides to God, and He is the same today. We get a warped view of Him when all we hear is, "God is love, God is love." It is true that God is love, but don't lose sight of the fact that God is also holy. He is righteous and He will judge. You are not rushing into heaven on the little love boat today. You will go to heaven only if you put your faith and trust in Jesus Christ, who shed His blood and gave His life on the cross. Then you will have eternal life and will be covered with the righteousness of Christ, standing complete and acceptable in Him. If you reject His salvation, there will be nothing left but judgment.

We have a warped view of God today. In this connection I always think of a judge who lived in west Texas many years ago. He had a reputation for making quick decisions. Other judges just didn't move as fast as he did. A friend asked him one day, "What is the secret of your making quick decisions?" "Well," he replied, "I'll tell you what I do. I just listen to the defense, and then I hand in a decision." The friend was startled. He asked the judge, "Don't you ever listen to the prosecution?" The judge said, "I used to, but that always confused me." And there are a lot of confused folks running around talking about the love of God, but we must never forget that He is also a God of judgment. Maybe that is the reason Ezekiel is a closed book, a sealed book to so many people. Liberal ministers encourage this by saying, "Nobody can understand the Book of Ezekiel." Well, you cannot understand it until you study it, that is for sure. We have had a remarkable principle laid down for us so far, and I hope we don't miss its message for us.

Now we come to the judging of the nations around Israel. I am not going to spend much time with them because they have long since passed off the stage, but they are important because they are to return. Only God can bring them back, and He says He will do that.

PROPHECY AGAINST THE AMMONITES

The Ammonites had a very bad beginning. They were a nomadic race descended from an incestuous relationship between Lot and his younger daughter (see Gen. 19:33–38). Their country lay along the Dead Sea. God said they would be made subject to Nebuchadnezzar, and they were.

Now God gives the reason for His judgment against them:

And say unto the Ammonites, Here the word of the Lord God; Thus saith the Lord God; Because thou saidst, Aha, against my sanctuary, when it was profaned; and against the land of Israel, when it was desolate; and against the house of Judah, when they went into captivity [Ezek. 25:3].

The Ammonites applauded the enemy that destroyed Israel. They were allies. But the same enemy destroyed Ammon. In Jeremiah 49:6 we read concerning them, "And afterward I will bring again the captivity of the children of Ammon, saith the Lord." God judged them so that they might know that He is the Lord.

Behold, therefore I will stretch out mine hand upon
thee, and will deliver thee for a spoil to the heathen; and
I will cut thee off from the people, and I will cause thee
to perish out of the countries: I will destroy thee; and
thou shalt know that I am the LORD [Ezek. 25:7].

PROPHECY AGAINST MOAB

The Moabites were more civilized than the Ammonites, but they, too,
were descended from an incestuous relationship—between Lot and
his older daughter (Gen. 19:33–38). Moab was situated on the east of
Israel but along the northern part of the Dead Sea. This is the land that
Ruth the Moabitess came from. She was an ancestor of King David,
which makes her also an ancestor of the Lord Jesus Christ—her name
appears in His genealogy (Matt. 1:5).

Notice the reason God will judge Moab:

Thus saith the Lord GOD; Because that Moab and Seir do
say, Behold, the house of Judah is like unto all the heathen;

Therefore, behold, I will open the side of Moab from the
cities, from his cities which are on his frontiers, the
glory of the country, Beth-jeshimoth, Baal-meon, and
Kiriathaim [Ezek. 25:8–9].

PROPHECY AGAINST EDOM

Edom is the nation that came from Esau, whose beginning is found
in Genesis 25. The little Book of Obadiah details the judgment against
Edom and the rock-hewn city of Petra. God gives His reason for judging Edom:

Thus saith the Lord GOD; Because that Edom hath dealt
against the house of Judah by taking vengeance, and
hath greatly offended, and revenged himself upon them;

Therefore thus saith the Lord GOD: I will also stretch out mine hand upon Edom, and will cut off man and beast from it; and I will make it desolate from Teman; and they of Dedan shall fall by the sword [Ezek. 25:12–13].

Edom's treatment of His chosen people is the cause of God's judgment.

PROPHECY AGAINST THE PHILISTINES

Thus saith the Lord GOD; Because the Philistines have dealt by revenge, and have taken vengeance with a despiteful heart, to destroy it for the old hatred;

Therefore thus saith the Lord GOD; Behold, I will stretch out mine hand upon the Philistines, and I will cut off the Cherethims, and destroy the remnant of the sea coast.

And I will execute great vengeance upon them with furious rebukes; and they shall know that I am the LORD, when I shall lay my vengeance upon them [Ezek. 25:15–17].

The Philistines have disappeared; they are no longer in that land. This judgment against them has been so literally fulfilled that the unbelieving critic wants to place Ezekiel's prophecy at a much later date so it can be considered history!

My friend, we will do well to take note of the fact that God judged the nations who had sinned against Him and His people.

CHAPTER 26

THEME: Judgment against Tyre

JUDGMENT AGAINST TYRE

Chapters 26—28 give us prophecies against Tyre and Sidon. Tyre and Sidon belong together like pork and beans, or ham and eggs. You never think of one without the other. These chapters are a marvelous example of the exactness of the literal fulfillment of prophecy.

Tyre was the capital of the great Phoenician nation which was famous for its seagoing traders. They plied the Mediterranean and even went beyond that. We know today that they went around the Pillars of Hercules and the Rock of Gibraltar, and into Great Britain, where they obtained tin. They established a colony in North Africa. Tarshish in Spain was founded by these people. They were great colonizers and went a lot farther than we used to think they did in their explorations.

Tyre was a great and proud city. Hiram, king of Tyre, had been a good friend of David and supplied him with building materials. Solomon and Hiram did not get along as well as David and Hiram had. Apparently Hiram was a great king. But, also, the center of Baal worship was there in Tyre and Sidon. Jezebel, the daughter of a king and former priest, married Ahab, king of Israel, and introduced Baal worship into the northern kingdom.

Now let's look at the tremendous prophecy God gives concerning Tyre and Sidon.

> **And it came to pass in the eleventh year, in the first day of the month, that the word of the LORD came unto me, saying,**
>
> **Son of man, because that Tyrus hath said against Jerusalem, Aha, she is broken that was the gates of the people: she is turned unto me: I shall be replenished, now she is laid waste [Ezek. 26:1–2].**

Tyre was destroyed at the same time Jerusalem was destroyed. Nebu-chadnezzar took Tyre.

Therefore thus saith the Lord God; Behold, I am against thee, O Tyrus, and will cause many nations to come up against thee, as the sea causeth his waves to come up [Ezek. 26:3].

When God says, "Behold, I am against thee," you can be sure He is against that place. Just as the waves break on the shore, God says, nations will come against Tyre, that great commercial center that had been invincible.

And they shall destroy the walls of Tyrus, and break down her towers: I will also scrape her dust from her, and make her like the top of a rock [Ezek. 26:4].

Nebuchadnezzar came against the city and destroyed it, but he didn't scrape it.

It shall be a place for the spreading of nets in the midst of the sea: for I have spoken it, saith the Lord God; and it shall become a spoil to the nations [Ezek. 26:5].

God said it would be a fishing village—not the proud commercial capital—and that is what it is today.

And her daughters which are in the field shall be slain by the sword; and they shall know that I am the Lord [Ezek. 26:6].

"Her daughters" are, I believe, the colonies that she established. She had established one on the island of Cyprus, by the way. Cyprus means "copper", and she obtained copper from there. The Phoenicians were the traders who brought these metals into the ancient civilized world.

> For thus saith the Lord God; Behold, I will bring upon
> Tyrus Nebuchadnezzar king of Babylon, a king of
> kings, from the north, with horses, and with chariots,
> and with horsemen, and companies, and much people.
>
> He shall slay with the sword thy daughters in the field:
> and he shall make a fort against thee, and cast a mount
> against thee, and lift up the buckler against thee.
>
> And he shall set engines of war against thy walls, and
> with his axes he shall break down thy towers.
>
> By reason of the abundance of his horses their dust shall
> cover thee: thy walls shall shake at the noise of the
> horsemen, and of the wheels, and of the chariots, when
> he shall enter into thy gates, as men enter into a city
> wherein is made a breach [Ezek. 26:7–10].

Nebuchadnezzar breached the walls of ancient Tyre just as he had at
Jerusalem, and this prophecy was literally fulfilled.

> With the hoofs of his horses shall he tread down all thy
> streets: he shall slay thy people by the sword, and thy
> strong garrisons shall go down to the ground [Ezek.
> 26:11].

It is very interesting to note that verses 7–11 clearly predict that Nebuchadnezzar will take the city, and the pronoun he is all through that section. But now, beginning with the next verse the pronoun changes to they. God had said that the nations were coming and here is that prediction:

> And they shall make a spoil of thy riches, and make a
> prey of thy merchandise: and they shall break down thy
> walls, and destroy thy pleasant houses: and they shall
> lay thy stones and thy timber and thy dust in the midst of
> the water.

And I will cause the noise of thy songs to cease; and the sound of thy harps shall be no more heard.

And I will make thee like the top of a rock: thou shalt be a place to spread nets upon; thou shalt be built no more: for I the LORD have spoken it, saith the Lord GOD [Ezek. 26:12–14].

Now this prophecy waited centuries for fulfillment. For three hundred years the ruins of Tyre lay there, and they were very impressive. Although Nebuchadnezzar had destroyed the city, this second prophecy had not been fulfilled. Who was going to take up the stones and even scrape the dust into the ocean?

Well, out of the west there comes Alexander the Great, symbolized as the he goat in Daniel's prophecy. You see, after the return of the Tyrians from Babylonian captivity, they decided to rebuild their city on an island and forget all about the mainland. Since they were a seafaring power, they could better protect themselves on an island. Well, when Alexander got there, he saw the ruins of the city, but the inhabited new city was out yonder on the island out of his reach. He had plenty of time and he had plenty of soldiers, so he decided to build a causeway to the city. Where did he get the material to construct it clear out there in the ocean? He took the building material of old Tyre, the stones, the pillars, and even the dust of the city, and built a causeway over which his army marched right into the new city of Tyre. He destroyed the city, and from that day to this it has never been rebuilt.

My friend, this is a remarkable prophecy! As I mentioned, the critics try to explain away the prophecy regarding Nebuchadnezzar's destruction of the city by saying that Ezekiel wrote it after it had happened, but it is impossible for them to claim that Ezekiel wrote after Alexander the Great! Only God can prophesy with such accuracy.

I have walked out on the isthmus that Alexander made from the mainland to the island and have seen the ruins. The ruins are being excavated and there were all kinds of broken pieces of pottery and artifacts around. Ezekiel's prophecy was literally fulfilled. You cannot look at the ruins of Tyre and say that the Word of God is guesswork.

Sidon stands today as it always has, but Tyre is gone. Nobody has tried to rebuild it. Lebanon hasn't tried. God's Word says that Tyre will never be rebuilt. If you can rebuild Tyre, you can contradict God's word, but I advise you to invest your money somewhere else.

CHAPTER 27

THEME: Lamentation for Tyre

LAMENTATION FOR TYRE

The preceding chapter gave us the prophecy concerning the destruction of Tyre, and we saw that the prophecy was literally fulfilled. The ruins of Tyre stand today as a witness to the accuracy of the Word of God. This was an impressive city in Ezekiel's day. Even though he may never have been there, he gives a lamentation for Tyre in this chapter. He laments the fact that this great city will fall. It was a *great* city— I don't want to minimize its beauty and magnificence. This is a sad and beautiful chapter in which Ezekiel likens Tyre, the capital of the Phoenician Empire, to a great ship that is wrecked. I cannot think of a better picture for seagoing people.

What was it that brought Tyre down?

> **The word of the LORD came again unto me, saying,**
>
> **Now, thou son of man, take up a lamentation for Tyrus;**
>
> **And say unto Tyrus, O thou that art situate at the entry of the sea, which art a merchant of the people for many isles, Thus saith the Lord GOD; O Tyrus, thou hast said, I am of perfect beauty [Ezek. 27:1–3].**

What brought Tyre down? The same thing that brought down the rock-hewn city of Petra also brought down the great city of Tyre: "The pride of thine heart hath deceived thee . . ." (Obad. 3). Pride in the glory, pomp, and prosperity is the thing that has brought down many great nations of the world and reduced them to ruins. This chapter speaks of how extensive the kingdom of Phoenicia was. It begins with Chittim (Cyprus), meaning copper, which was one of their colonies, and extends all the way to Tarshish, which means smelting plant or refinery. Tarshish was sort of a jumping-off place for the Phoenicians.

Jonah bought a ticket to that city, but he never saw it—instead he saw the interior of a big fish!

The ships of Tarshish did sing of thee in thy market: and thou wast replenished, and made very glorious in the midst of the seas [Ezek. 27:25].

Tyre was a great commercial center. Merchants came from all over the world to buy and sell. You could find just about anything you wanted in Tyre. In verse 17 it says that Israel traded in her markets. "Minnith" was perhaps olives or figs made into some kind of preserves. You could buy anything and everything in the markets of Tyre.

If you want a picture of Tyre as the great commercial center, you will see it depicted in a prophecy of Babylon in the future when it will become the commercial, religious, and political center of the world. It will be the capital of the Antichrist. "The merchandise of gold, and silver, and precious stones, and of pearls, and fine linen, and purple, and silk, and scarlet, and all thyine wood, and all manner vessels of ivory, and all manner vessels of most precious wood, and of brass, and iron, and marble, and cinnamon, and odours, and ointments, and frankincense, and wine, and oil, and fine flour, and wheat, and beasts, and sheep, and horses, and chariots, and slaves, and souls of men. And the fruits that thy soul lusted after . . ." (Rev. 18:12–14).

This also is a picture of London, Paris, Rome, New York City, and Los Angeles. You can buy anything you want in these cities. If you have the money, you can buy it. Today is the age of materialism, just as it was in the days of Tyre.

Tyre was like a great ship. Everything the people needed was on board, and the music was playing. There was laughter, and the wine and champagne flowed. It was all there. Then it all disappeared. God judged it. Now here is the lamentation and the weeping over that great city. That is exactly what is going to happen in the last days. In those last days the stock market will fail, and everything you have in your safe deposit boxes won't be worth a dime, and everything you thought was valuable will suddenly become dust and ashes in your hands.

What a tragic day it was when Tyre fell; what a tragic day it will be when the same thing happens in the future!

Be careful. Don't put all of your eggs in one basket. I think people ought to enjoy the affluent society we have today. I see nothing wrong in it, provided it does not become an obsession or an idol. Unfortunately, it has become that to many folk. Even in many of our good churches there is really very little Bible teaching. We play games. We pat each other on the back, and we have "fellowship"—we love to talk about that. And we quote a Bible verse now and then to make sure we are religious and pious, and we go through the little ceremonies of the church. They did that in Tyre; they did it in Jerusalem, and God destroyed them. He destroyed them because they had an opportunity, a privilege, and a responsibility that they shrugged off.

And in their wailing they shall take up a lamentation for thee, and lament over thee, saying, What city is like Tyrus, like the destroyed in the midst of the sea? [Ezek. 27:32].

Tyre was like a great ship that had gone down at sea.

In the time when thou shalt be broken by the seas in the depths of the waters thy merchandise and all thy company in the midst of thee shall fall [Ezek. 27:34].

All will be swallowed up by the sea.

The merchants among the people shall hiss at thee; thou shalt be a terror, and never shalt be any more [Ezek. 27:36].

As I walked through the ruins of Tyre I heard no music nor laughter. I could not see the buildings or the gold and silver. All I saw were broken pieces of pottery and the wreck and ruin of what had once been a great city. And the God of heaven says, "I judged you." There must be a message in this picture of Tyre for our day and generation.

CHAPTER 28

THEME: Judgment against the prince of Tyre; judgment against the king

JUDGMENT AGAINST THE PRINCE OF TYRE

In this chapter we find the judgment of the prince and king of Tyre and Sidon. The prophecy looks beyond the local ruler to the one who is behind the kingdoms of the world—Satan.

The word of the Lord came again unto me, saying,

Son of man, say unto the prince of Tyrus, Thus saith the Lord God; Because thine heart is lifted up, and thou hast said, I am a God, I sit in the seat of God, in the midst of the seas; yet thou art a man, and not God, though thou set thine heart as the heart of God [Ezek. 28:1-2].

Again the word of the Lord comes to Ezekiel, and this time there are two messages: one for the prince of Tyre and one for the king of Tyre. In back of the great kingdom, the great commercial center, the great political center, and the great stronghold of Tyre, we are going to find the one who apparently also controls all the kingdoms of this world. He is Satan. He offered the kingdoms of the world to the Lord Jesus during his temptation in the wilderness: "And the devil, taking him up into a high mountain, shewed unto him all the kingdoms of the world in a moment of time. And the devil said unto him, All this power will I give thee, and the glory of them: for that is delivered unto me; and to whomsoever I will give it. If thou therefore wilt worship me, all shall be thine" (Luke 4:5-7). The Lord rejected Satan's offer, but not because He didn't recognize his ownership—Christ knew that Satan did have the kingdoms. Ultimately Christ will rule over the kingdoms of the world—but not as the vice-regent of Satan! Today, however, the Devil is still the prince of the power of the air. He is the one who is in back of the kingdoms of our world, whether we like it or not.

Here is, I believe, a type of Antichrist. Actually, it takes two persons to fulfill all that Scripture says about the Antichrist (and John says there are many). One will deny the Person of Christ—be His enemy; the other will imitate Him. There will be a religious ruler and a political ruler. Now here in Ezekiel we have, I believe, the combination set before us.

This is the vice-regent of Satan: "Because thine heart is lifted up, and thou hast said, I am a God"—this is exactly what the Antichrist is going to say. The apostle Paul says this of him: "Who opposeth and exalteth himself above all that is called God, or that is worshipped; so that he as God sitteth in the temple of God, shewing himself that he is God" (2 Thess. 2:4). And this prince of Tyre says, "I sit in the seat of God, in the midst of the seas."

But God says, "Yet thou art a man, and not God, though thou set thine heart as the heart of God."

Behold, thou art wiser than Daniel; there is no secret that they can hide from thee [Ezek. 28:3].

Here is another reference to Daniel. Ezekiel and Daniel, you remember, were contemporaries. This young man Ezekiel had great respect for Daniel, who was prime minister in Babylon, and who really stood for the Lord. I personally think that Ezekiel had the hardest job. He lived with and preached to the captives. As I said earlier, I would have much preferred to live in the palace and spend one night in the lions' den than to work with the captives, but Ezekiel had no choice in the matter.

Ezekiel refers to Daniel's wisdom. Ezekiel says that this prince of Tyre was a smart boy. If you don't think there were wise men in that day, you are wrong. I think the wise men in that day would make the so-called intellectual crowd that centers in Harvard today look like beginners in kindergarten. These great men in Ezekiel's day were really *wise* men.

Now I believe that this prince of Tyre represents the religious ruler aspect of the Antichrist. And I think he comes out of Israel. You see, the Antichrist, the political ruler, comes out of the sea of the nations of the world. I think he will be a Gentile. His advisor, the religious ruler, will come out of the land. The religious ruler will be like a prime minister to the political ruler, like Daniel was in Babylon, or like Joseph in Egypt, or Disraeli in England. Perhaps I should not make that kind of comparison, but I think it serves to illustrate the two positions.

JUDGMENT AGAINST THE KING

Moreover the word of the LORD came unto me, saying [Ezek. 28:11].

Ezekiel is not going to let anyone forget that he is not giving his own opinion, but he is telling forth God's message.

We have had a lamentation of the city of Tyre. We have talked about the prince of Tyre, and now we come to a lamentation of the king of Tyre. Immediately we pass beyond the local king of Tyre—there were many of them. It wasn't safe to be a king in those days. Uneasy lies the head that wears the crown. The glory did not last long. It was like the bromide *sic transit gloria mundi,* which is Latin for "thus passeth the glory of the world."

The king in back of the kingdom of Tyre is Satan. Ezekiel 28 is one of the few passages in the Word of God that gives us the origin of the Devil and of evil. I don't want to press this too much, but read carefully these words—

Son of man, take up a lamentation upon the king of Tyrus, and say unto him, Thus saith the Lord GOD; Thou sealest up the sum, full of wisdom, and perfect in beauty [Ezek. 28:12].

Satan was the wisest creature God ever created. Keep in mind that Satan is a created being. He was created perfect in beauty. If you think of Satan as a creature with horns, a forked tail, and cloven feet, you are wrong. You have been reading the literature of the Middle Ages which has its origin in Greek mythology that goes back into Asia Minor. There was a great temple of Apollo in Pergamum; also there was one in Corinth, and in Ephesus, just to name a few. This is a description of the god Pan, or Bacchus, the god of pleasure. He has horns, he runs through the grape vineyard, he is the god of the grape, the god of wine. From his waist down he is represented as a goat. The creature with horns, a forked tail, and cloven feet is right out of Greek mythology.

The Word of God does not present Satan in that manner. The Bible presents him as perfect in beauty. If you could see him, you would find that he is the most beautiful creature you have ever seen. I have heard many people say how good-looking the men of certain cults are. When I was a boy, I heard such a man. He was in one of the cults. He had silver gray hair and was a fine looking man—in fact, he was very handsome. Some women would almost swoon at his presence. People treated him as if he were a god, a claim that he almost made. Do you know what he was? He was a minister of Satan; I don't mind saying it. When I was a boy, with no instruction in the things of God, he almost led me astray. Oh, how terrible the ministers of Satan are!

Paul has something to say about the ministers of Satan. "For such are false apostles, deceitful workers, transforming themselves into the apostles of Christ. And no marvel; for Satan himself is transformed into an angel of light. Therefore it is no great thing if his ministers also be transformed as the ministers of righteousness . . ." (2 Cor. 11:13–15).

Ezekiel says of this one: "Thou sealest up the sum, full of wisdom, and perfect in beauty." What was it that brought him down? We will see that when we come to verse 15.

Thou hast been in Eden the garden of God; every precious stone was thy covering, the sardius, topaz, and the diamond, the beryl, the onyx, and the jasper, the sapphire, the emerald, and the carbuncle, and gold: the workmanship of thy tabrets and of thy pipes was prepared in thee in the day that thou wast created [Ezek. 28:13].

"Thou hast been in Eden the garden of God"—no king of Tyre has been in the Garden of Eden!

"Every precious stone was thy covering"—can you imagine what a beautiful creature he was!

"The workmanship of thy tabrets and of thy pipes was prepared in thee." Not only could he sing, he was a band; he was music itself. Do you know the origin of music on this earth? Go back to Genesis 4:21, and you will see that it originated with the progeny of Cain. And when I hear some of the music of my contemporaries, I am confident that it came out of the pit—it couldn't come from any place else! Satan was a musician.

> **Thou art the anointed cherub that covereth; and I have set thee so: thou wast upon the holy mountain of God; thou hast walked up and down in the midst of the stones of fire [Ezek. 28:14].**

Satan was the "anointed cherub that covereth"—that is, he protected the throne of God. This is not the Eden which was on earth, but apparently is a picture of heaven itself. Satan had access to heaven, of course.

> **Thou wast perfect in thy ways from the day that thou wast created, till iniquity was found in thee [Ezek. 28:15].**

Satan protected God's throne. He had the highest position a created being could have. What was it that brought him down? Ezekiel doesn't tell us, but Isaiah 14:12–15 has already told us: "How art thou fallen from heaven, O Lucifer, son of the morning! how art thou cut down to the ground, which didst weaken the nations! For thou hast said in thine heart, I will ascend into heaven, I will exalt my throne above the stars of God: I will sit also upon the mount of the congregation, in the sides of the north: I will ascend above the heights of the clouds; I will be like the most High. Yet thou shalt be brought down to hell, to the sides of the pit." The thing that brought him down was *pride!* Satan wanted to lift up his throne. He wanted to divorce himself from God and be God. He was in rebellion against God.

Now, let me say this: If you are one of the saints today who thinks you have arrived, that you are perfect, and you have set yourself up as a standard, remember that Satan was the angel of light; he was perfect—but he fell. Since *he* fell, what about you? What about me? We are only frail human beings.

God cannot tolerate rebellion, so what is He going to do?

> **By the multitude of thy merchandise they have filled the midst of thee with violence, and thou hast sinned: therefore I will cast thee as profane out of the mountain of God: and I will destroy thee, O covering cherub, from the midst of the stones of fire [Ezek. 28:16].**

Satan will be judged for his sin. He is only a creature. I don't know about you, but this is comforting to me. I frankly would not be able to overcome him. I am no match for him. I am thankful, therefore, that God is going to deal with him.

> **Thine heart was lifted up because of thy beauty, thou hast corrupted thy wisdom by reason of thy brightness: I will cast thee to the ground, I will lay thee before kings, that they may behold thee [Ezek. 28:17].**

"Thine heart was lifted up because of thy beauty"—pride.

"Thou hast corrupted thy wisdom by reason of thy brightness." You see, Solomon, the wisest man, played the fool. And here we see that the greatest creature whom God ever created, perfect (filled with all that could be learned), played the fool. Oh, my friend, God's children can do the same today!

"I will cast thee to the ground, I will lay thee before kings, that they may behold thee." God is going to make a spectacle of Satan someday.

**All they that know thee among the people shall be aston-
ished at thee: thou shalt be a terror, and never shalt thou
be any more [Ezek. 28:19].**

At some time in the future God is going to get rid of Satan in His
universe, and we pray for that day to come.

In verses 20–24 judgment is pronounced on Sidon, but not complete destruction. He says that there will be blood in the streets, and
that is exactly what happened. It is a matter of history. It is interesting
to note that Tyre, the prominent city and capital city, was destroyed,
scraped like a rock, never to be rebuilt; yet Sidon, about fifteen miles
from Tyre, was also judged, but not destroyed. That city exists today;
it is the place where oil is brought in from the Near East. It comes by
pipeline and is loaded onto ships. Sidon is a thriving port, whereas
down the coast is Tyre lying in ruins, with only a little fishing village
there. God says that Tyre will never be rebuilt. God knew what He was
talking about. In this chapter He has made the prophecies clear-cut:
Tyre would be destroyed and never be rebuilt; Sidon would be judged
but not destroyed. Today after approximately twenty-five hundred
years, Tyre is gone and Sidon lives on.

**Thus saith the Lord God; When I shall have gathered the
house of Israel from the people among whom they are
scattered, and shall be sanctified in them in the sight of
the heathen, then shall they dwell in their land that I
have given to my servant Jacob.**

**And they shall dwell safely therein, and shall build
houses, and plant vineyards; yea, they shall dwell with
confidence, when I have executed judgments upon all
those that despise them round about them; and they
shall know that I am the Lord their God [Ezek.
28:25–26].**

God says, "I intend to regather Israel." Satan cannot disturb His plan
and program with the children of Israel. Neither can any theologian

today dismiss God's plan to restore Israel to the land in peace. One reason that so many theologians are believed when they say that God is through with the nation Israel is because God's people are not acquainted with Isaiah, Jeremiah, Ezekiel, Daniel, and the minor prophets. The theme song of these prophets is that God is *not* through with Israel as a nation. For this reason they should be studied. They throw new light on the Word of God so that it is no longer a jigsaw puzzle, but everything falls into place.

CHAPTERS 29 AND 30

THEME: Prophecy against Egypt, lamentation for
Egypt

PROPHECY AGAINST EGYPT

Many conservative commentators take the position that the prophecies concerning Egypt are of more interest than the one concerning Tyre. I must confess that I do not concur in that—the prophecies concerning Tyre are remarkable. Also, the ones concerning Egypt are interesting, and we will find a remarkable prophecy in this chapter. Egypt was a great nation, and it had not been destroyed. It had maintained its integrity down through the centuries. It was one of the most ancient nations. It did not need to put up a wall of defense. After all, the desert was a pretty good defense. There was only one entrance, and that was through the Nile River valley. All Egypt had to do for protection was put up a good defense there. You will find that the cities of Egypt were not walled—walls were not necessary.

Now God says that the Egyptians will go into captivity for forty years.

> **In the tenth year, in the tenth month, in the twelfth day of the month, the word of the LORD came unto me, saying,**
>
> **Son of man, set thy face against Pharaoh king of Egypt, and prophesy against him, and against all Egypt [Ezek. 29:1–2].**

God takes a very definite position against the land of Egypt. It was this nation that had reduced His people to slavery in the brickyards and had introduced them to idolatry. Egypt had been a thorn in the flesh of Israel for years; yet Israel was constantly running to Egypt for help. For some reason the children of Israel seemed to lean upon Egypt. Now God says He is against Egypt and it will be destroyed.

Speak, and say, Thus saith the Lord GOD; Behold, I am against thee, Pharaoh king of Egypt, the great dragon that lieth in the midst of his rivers, which hath said, My river is mine own, and I have made it for myself [Ezek. 29:3].

The crocodile, apparently, is the "great dragon" or sea monster here. Pharaoh is likened unto the crocodile that says, "This is my river." It is interesting to note that Egypt worshiped all manner of birds, beasts, and bugs. You will notice that the plagues against Egypt (Exod. 7—11) were leveled against the gods which Egypt worshiped. I think that in spite of how terrible the plagues were, they also reveal that God has a sense of humor. Imagine worshiping Heka, the frog-headed goddess, and then waking up one morning and finding frogs all over your bedroom. What are you going to do? Start killing off your goddess? I think the Lord must have smiled at that.

The Pharaoh mentioned here is Pharaoh Hophra, also called Apries in the Greek. He was the grandson of Pharaoh Nechoh, who defeated king Josiah in Judah at Megiddo; in fact, Josiah was slain in that battle. Kings Jehoiakim, Jehoiachin, and Zedekiah all turned to Pharaoh Hophra when Jerusalem was besieged. The Egyptian army came up, went through Phoenicia, and forced the Chaledeans to raise the siege of Jerusalem. The prophet Jeremiah announced the doom of Pharaoh Hophra: "The LORD of hosts, the God of Israel, saith; Behold, I will punish the multitude of No, and Pharaoh, and Egypt, with their gods, and their kings; even Pharaoh, and all them that trust in him: And I will deliver them into the hand of those that seek their lives, and into the hand of Nebuchadnezzar king of Babylon, and into the hand of his servants: and afterward it shall be inhabited, as in the days of old, saith the LORD" (Jer. 46:25–26).

You may find it interesting to note that the critic has made an issue of the fact that the prophecy of the destruction of Egypt was not fulfilled at this time. It was fulfilled seventeen years later. However, if you read the prophecy carefully, you will see that although the prophecy was given through Ezekiel at this time, nothing is said about immediate fulfillment. Egypt was destroyed seventeen years later as God said it would be.

Now notice what God says will happen to Egypt:

> **Yet thus saith the Lord God; At the end of forty years will I gather the Egyptians from the people whither they were scattered [Ezek. 29:13].**

Seventeen years later, to be exact, the king of Babylon, Nebuchadnezzar, came and took the Egyptians into captivity. They were in captivity for forty years, not seventy years like Israel.

> **And I will bring again the captivity of Egypt, and will cause them to return into the land of Pathros, into the land of their habitation; and they shall be there a base kingdom [Ezek. 29:14].**

Now notice carefully this next verse—

> **It shall be the basest of the kingdoms; neither shall it exalt itself any more above the nations: for I will diminish them, that they shall no more rule over the nations [Ezek. 29:15].**

Egypt had been the great power of the ancient world. They came out of the dawn of history as a great nation. Their monuments and tombs reveal the fact that they had a civilization that was second to none. It is believed today by many historians that the Greeks got a great deal of their information from the Egyptians. Egypt was a great nation, but God said, "I am going to let Nebuchadnezzar take you. Not only that, you are going to be in captivity for forty years, and at the end of that time you are going to return to your land, but you are going to be a base kingdom—in fact, the basest of the kingdoms." My friend, on our tours we visit many lands in the Near East, and we can see how accurate God's prediction was. No one can go to Cairo without his heart being sick when he sees the poverty and the low levels to which the people have sunk.

> Therefore thus saith the Lord GOD; Behold, I will give the land of Egypt unto Nebuchadnezzar king of Babylon; and he shall take her multitude, and take her spoil, and take her prey; and it shall be the wages for his army.

> I have given him the land of Egypt for his labour wherewith he served against it, because they wrought for me, saith the Lord GOD [Ezek. 29:19–20].

Babylon, you see, was to conquer all these nations—including Tyre, Egypt, and, of course, Israel. Babylon was the first great empire.

LAMENTATION FOR EGYPT

This brings us to chapter 30, which is considered a lamentation. Ezekiel speaks of the desolation of Egypt, and it is indeed a desolate nation.

> The word of the LORD came again unto me, saying [Ezek. 30:1].

Here we go again. This phrase has been repeated I don't know how many times. Ezekiel doesn't want there to be a doubt in any mind whose word this is.

> Son of man, prophesy and say, Thus saith the Lord GOD; Howl ye, Woe worth the day! [Ezek. 30:2].

This is a time of wailing and mourning, a lamentation.

> For the day is near, even the day of the LORD is near, a cloudy day; it shall be the time of the heathen [Ezek. 30:3].

A cloudy day was unusual. They don't have many clouds in the land of Egypt because they have less than an inch of rain in that section. They depend upon the river Nile for the water they need. By the way, they worshiped the crocodile of the Nile, as well as everything else in the animal world.

"The time of the heathen" is better translated the time of the *nations,* and we are certainly living in that day when the nations are really stirring throughout the world.

> **And the sword shall come upon Egypt, and great pain shall be in Ethiopia, when the slain shall fall in Egypt, and they shall take away her multitude, and her foundations shall be broken down [Ezek. 30:4].**

At times there was an alliance between Egypt and Ethiopia, although a great deal of the time there was enmity and warfare between the two nations. It is believed by many conservative scholars that Moses, when he was Pharaoh's daughter's son, would have been the next Pharaoh, and that he actually led an expedition against Ethiopia.

> **Ethiopia, and Libya, and Lydia, and all the mingled people, and Chub, and the men of the land that is in league, shall fall with them by the sword [Ezek. 30:5].**

At this time there was an alliance among these nations, but they would all become subject to Nebuchadnezzar, who was actually a world ruler. In fact, he is the head of gold in Daniel's prophecy (ch. 2) of the four great world kingdoms.

> **Thus saith the Lord; They also that uphold Egypt shall fall; and the pride of her power shall come down: from the tower of Syene shall they fall in it by the sword, saith the Lord God [Ezek. 30:6].**

Not only Israel, but all of these other nations had looked to Egypt for help, and they will all be judged together.

> And I will make the rivers dry, and sell the land into the
> hand of the wicked: and I will make the land waste, and
> all that is therein, by the hand of strangers: I the LORD
> have spoken it [Ezek. 30:12].

These rivers, as we have seen before, are actually the different branches down in the delta of the Nile, and there were many of them. There were also canals in that very rich fertile area. Near there was the land of Goshen, where the Israelites settled when they first came to Egypt.

"I will make the rivers dry, and sell the land into the hand of the wicked." Egypt fell later on to Alexander the Great, and when he died his generals took over the nations he had conquered. Cleopatra, who was not an Egyptian but a Greek, ruled over Egypt.

"I will make the land waste, and all that is therein, by the hand of strangers." "Strangers" are foreigners. Egypt came under the control of foreign nations, and the canals were allowed to fill up. Although I have never gotten into that delta section, a friend of mine whom I met in Cairo had just come from there, and he told me that it is really a swamp in that section. God had said that He would make the land waste, and that is what it is today.

Now here is another remarkable prophecy—

> Thus saith the Lord GOD; I will also destroy the idols,
> and I will cause their images to cease out of Noph; and
> there shall be no more a prince of the land of Egypt: and
> I will put a fear in the land of Egypt [Ezek. 30:13].

"I will cause their images to cease out of Noph." Noph is Memphis, and in Ezekiel's time it was the great city of Egypt. It was a very wealthy city, and it had idols in profusion—up and down both sides of the streets were idol after idol. They were the city's decoration! No other place has ever had idols like Memphis had them. Here God says that He would make the idols to cease out of Memphis.

I have walked over what is supposed to be the ruins of Memphis, and all that is left of the idols is one great big statue of Raamses. It lies on its back, and a building has been erected around it to house the statue. That is the only thing left in Memphis. God did exactly what He said He was going to do. He made the idols to cease.

"There shall be no more a prince of the land of Egypt." There is no royal line in Egypt any more. Neither can any of the rulers be called great men. They all have had to look to other nations for aid and support.

> **And I will pour my fury upon Sin, the strength of Egypt; and I will cut off the multitude of No [Ezek. 30:15].**

"I will pour out my fury upon Sin"—which is Pelusium, now completely buried in the sand.

"I will cut off the multitude of No"—this is Thebes, which was a great city in the upper Nile. The ruins are there, but its greatness is all gone.

In the next verses God continues to speak of these great cities of Egypt which have now disappeared altogether.

> **Son of man, I have broken the arm of Pharaoh king of Egypt; and, lo, it shall not be bound up to be healed, to put a roller to bind it, to make it strong to hold the sword.**

> **Therefore thus saith the Lord God; Behold, I am against Pharaoh king of Egypt, and will break his arms, the strong, and that which was broken; and I will cause the sword to fall out of his hand [Ezek. 30:21–22].**

God states once again that Egypt will fall. The pictures of Egyptian rules always show them holding the scepter in their hands. The scepter was a token of their power. God says, "I have broken the arm of Pharaoh." It is hard to hold a scepter with a broken arm! And God goes on to say, "It shall not be bound up to be healed." Babylon was going to conquer Egypt, and Pharaoh would be powerless to stop it. All of this was literally fulfilled.

CHAPTERS 31 AND 32

THEME: Judgment against Pharaoh; Pharaoh's greatness and glory; Pharaoh's fall; lamentation over the fall

JUDGMENT AGAINST PHARAOH

These two chapters conclude the section regarding the judgment of Egypt (chapters 29—32). It is interesting that Ezekiel devotes four chapters to Egypt and also Isaiah and Jeremiah and the minor prophets deal with Egypt. Egypt looms large in the history of the nation Israel. It is rather ironic that Egypt is such a thorn in the flesh to Israel at the present time. Egypt, in fact, is a dog in the manger. Israel didn't want the Baby in the manger, so it got the dog in the manger!

In chapter 31 we see the fall of Pharaoh. It is described in a parabolic form and represents both Pharaoh and his subjects. Verses 1–9 give the greatness and glory of Pharaoh in Egypt; verses 10–14 give the fall of Egypt in the parable of the tree; and verses 15–18 give the lamentation over the fall of the tree and the crisis which came to the nations of the world because of it. It had the same effect in that day as it would at the present time if the United States were destroyed overnight. That would certainly change the situation in the world, I am sure.

I trust you have seen how important the Book of Ezekiel is. It is a book that reveals the glory of the Lord and the fact that our God is a holy God who will judge sin. Now God is merciful, and He is kind. He loves mankind; He wants to save the human family, and He is not willing that any should perish, but He also judges sin. He intends to judge, and He will not spare you if you reject His gracious offer.

That is what happened to Israel, and that is what happened to Egypt. Egypt was judged on the basis of the light she had, and she had been given a great deal of light.

THE GREATNESS AND GLORY OF PHARAOH

Son of man, speak unto Pharaoh king of Egypt, and to his multitude; Whom art thou like in thy greatness? [Ezek. 31:2].

God recognized the greatness of Egypt—probably over a couple of millenniums this vast kingdom had dominated the world. It was the breadbasket for the world because it did not have to depend on the rainfall. The Nile River overflowed each year to water their crops. It was a nation of tremendous power.

Behold, the Assyrian was a cedar in Lebanon with fair branches, and with a shadowing shroud, and of an high stature; and his top was among the thick boughs [Ezek. 31:3].

God says, "I liken Assyria, that great nation in the north, to a great cedar tree." Now there is more than one tree in a forest because one tree won't make a forest. Assyria stood way above the other trees and dominated. But God brought Assyria down. This message should have gotten through to Pharaoh and his people. Pharaoh, too, is a great tree. He has dominated everything. The people of Egypt are great, but now they are going to be brought low. As we saw in chapter 29, Egypt is going to become a base kingdom. Well, for a period of over two thousand years now it has been a base kingdom. It will never be a world empire again.

THE FALL OF PHARAOH

Therefore thus saith the Lord GOD; Because thou hast lifted up thyself in height, and he hath shot up his top among the thick boughs, and his heart is lifted up in his height [Ezek. 31:10].

The phrase, "Therefore thus saith the Lord God," indicates the divisions in this chapter. In this division we see that Pharaoh is lifted up in pride. Pride is in the human heart, and his greatness blinded him to the danger that he was in.

> **I have therefore delivered him into the hand of the mighty one of the heathen; he shall surely deal with him: I have driven him out for his wickedness [Ezek. 31:11].**

At this point in history who is the mighty one of the nations? It is Nebuchadnezzar, king of Babylon. I don't think Ezekiel is speaking about Satan because Satan has had Egypt for years, so this wasn't something new. If you want to confirm the fact that this "mighty one" was Nebuchadnezzar, read the Book of Daniel. Daniel said to king Nebuchadnezzar, "You are the head of gold"—the greatness of this man has not been exceeded.

"I have therefore delivered him," he is talking about Pharaoh of Egypt. God is going to deal with him; He is going to drive him out because of his wickedness.

> **And strangers, the terrible of the nations, have cut him off, and have left him: upon the mountains and in all the valleys his branches are fallen, and his boughs are broken by all the rivers of the land; and all the people of the earth are gone down from his shadow, and have left him [Ezek. 31:12].**

Egypt would be taken, and it would be a shock to the world.

LAMENTATION OVER THE FALL OF PHARAOH

This is a very remarkable section of the Word of God. If you are a student of the Word, I recommend that you spend a great deal of time here.

> Thus saith the Lord GOD; In the day when he went down
> to the grave I caused a mourning: I covered the deep for
> him, and I restrained the floods thereof, and the great
> waters were stayed: and I caused Lebanon to mourn for
> him, and all the trees of the field fainted for him [Ezek.
> 31:15].

The word "grave" in this verse is *sheol*. This verse speaks of Pharaoh who is going to go down in defeat and be killed. Sheol, although at times does mean the grave, means here the unseen world, the unknown region, or the abode of the dead—not just the grave where the physical body is placed after death. It is the place where the spirit goes. You remember that Solomon spoke about the fact that the body returns to the earth, and the spirit goes to God: "Then shall the dust return to the earth as it was: and the spirit shall return unto God who gave it" (Eccl. 12:7). The human body is nothing in the world but dust. Speaking of man the psalmist says, "For he [God] knoweth our frame; he remembereth that we are dust" (Ps. 103:14). Sometimes we forget we are only dust, and when dust gets stuck on itself, it becomes mud! We need to remember that as far as our bodies are concerned, they are dust. When we put our bodies in the ground, they will go back to dust. The Lord Jesus spoke of the fact that when a believer dies his body sleeps. And Paul speaks of the physical body as sleeping in 1 Thessalonians 4:13.

Where do the spirits of the lost go? They, too, go to sheol, the unseen world. We know from a parable—which is also a true-life story which Jesus told (Luke 16:19–31) about two men who died—that sheol is divided into two compartments. One is called the place of torment, and that is where the rich man went. The other is called Abraham's Bosom, which is the place where the beggar went when he died. The place of torment is not to be confused with hell or the lake of fire of the New Testament. Apparently sheol was a temporary "abode of the dead," as the Lord Jesus emptied the section called paradise or Abraham's Bosom when he ascended (Eph. 4:8–10). The section called the place of torment will not be emptied until all who are there will stand before the Great White Throne for their final judgment (Rev. 20:11–15).

With this background in mind, notice that Ezekiel gives a picture of Pharaoh going down into sheol. Remember that God is not speaking of Pharaoh's body here. The grave receives the bodies, but the immaterial part of man, that which has endless being, goes to sheol.

"I covered the deep for him, and I restrained the floods thereof, and the great waters were stayed: and I caused Lebanon to mourn for him." When he died, the entire world mourned. Up there in Lebanon, which was in the great nation of Phoenicia, there was great mourning. The nations of the world mourned when Egypt went down. All were dependent upon it—their economy rested upon it, and its allies were protected by it. What a picture this is!

> **I made the nations to shake at the sound of his fall, when I cast him down to hell with them that descend into the pit: and all the trees of Eden, the choice and best of Lebanon, all that drink water, shall be comforted in the nether parts of the earth [Ezek. 31:16].**

"When I cast him down to hell [sheol] with them that descend into the pit [the grave]." Now the tree, representing Pharaoh, is cut down. And where does Pharaoh go? To sheol. Now notice what he discovers:

> **To whom art thou thus like in glory and in greatness among the trees of Eden? yet shalt thou be brought down with the trees of Eden unto the nether [lower] parts of the earth: thou shalt lie in the midst of the uncircumcised with them that be slain by the sword. This is Pharaoh and all his multitude, saith the Lord God [Ezek. 31:18].**

When Pharaoh got to sheol, he found other rulers that had been slain were there too.

He discovered something else: there is democracy in death. We talk a great deal today about integration. There is nothing that will integrate the rich and the poor, the black and the white, the male and the female, those at the top of the social ladder and those at the bottom of it, like *death!* Death will bring them all to the same level, not only the placing of their bodies in the grave, but also their spirits.

Probably one of the startling things to some people will be the realization that they haven't died as an animal dies. An atheist said to me, "When a man dies it is just like a dog that dies. He simply ceases to exist. There is no life after death." Well, he is going to be surprised when he moves into sheol and finds out who all is there. It will be quite a company of people who did not believe that there was an afterlife or a judgment to come. They will all be on the same par. This is total integration! The spirits of all those who have rejected the Lord Jesus will be there—not because they are sinners but because they have rejected Christ as their Savior. It is the sin of *rejecting Christ* that will take them to sheol and finally to the Great White Throne of judgment and the lake of fire. The Lord Jesus made this clear when He said, "Of sin, because they believe not on me" (John 16:9). How terrible it is not to trust Christ as your Savior.

This passage of Scripture opens up a new area altogether. Someone has called this the "Dante's Inferno of the Bible." And it is like that. The lost do go to a definite *place.* The Lord Jesus called it a place of torment and a place where the lost wait for judgment. Some people say, "Oh, I am going to appear before God all right, but I will get things straightened out there because I have been a pretty good fellow." But when they stand in the presence of the One who was crucified for them, they are going to find out that their puny works did not amount to much. They will discover that they have a fallen nature with no capacity for God, and no interest in Him at all. Where else could God put them? Do you think He could take anyone to heaven with Him who is in rebellion against Him? My friend, this is a very important passage of Scripture.

In chapter 32 the lamentation continues—

Son of man, take up a lamentation for Pharaoh king of Egypt, and say unto him, Thou art like a young lion of the nations, and thou art as a whale in the seas: and

thou camest forth with thy rivers, and troubledst the waters with thy feet, and fouledst their rivers [Ezek. 32:2].

"Thou art as a whale in the seas" is better translated "thou art like a monster, the crocodile." The Egyptians worshiped both the lion and the crocodile.

"Thou camest forth with thy rivers, and troubledst the waters with thy feet, and fouledst their rivers." You see, back there they had an ecology problem. Old Pharaoh was muddying the water.

Thus saith the Lord God; I will therefore spread out my net over thee with a company of many people; and they shall bring thee up in my net [Ezek. 32:3].

"Thus saith the Lord God; I will therefore spread out my net over thee"—"just as you put nets in the Nile River to get fish, that's the way I am going to catch you, you monster of the Nile River, you crocodile!" It is as if God is saying, "I am going to pull you out and move you to a place where you won't live in a palace. You will find yourself on the same plane with your subjects." Death surely does level out humanity, does it not?

For thus saith the Lord God; The sword of the king of Babylon shall come upon thee [Ezek. 32:11].

The king of Babylon will take Egypt.

Son of man, wail for the multitude of Egypt, and cast them down, even her, and the daughters of the famous nations, unto the nether parts of the earth, with them that go down into the pit.

Whom dost thou pass in beauty? go down, and be thou laid with the uncircumcised [Ezek. 32:18–19].

Now Pharaoh will find that the other rulers are down there in sheol—

> **Asshur is there and all her company: his graves are about him: all of them slain, fallen by the sword [Ezek. 32:22].**

"Asshur" is Assyria. And he finds somebody else is there—

> **There is Elam and all her multitude round about her grave, all of them slain, fallen by the sword, which are gone down uncircumcised into the nether parts of the earth, which caused their terror in the land of the living; yet have they borne their shame with them that go down to the pit [Ezek. 32:24].**

"There is Elam and all her multitude round about her grave." You see, the body was put in the grave, but *they* have gone to another place, to sheol, the unseen world. Our Lord Jesus called it the place of torment for those who are lost. The saved are in the section which He called Abraham's Bosom; then later to the repentant thief on the cross He called it paradise: "Today thou shalt be with me in paradise."

Here are others Pharaoh finds in sheol—

> **There is Meshech, Tubal, and all her multitude: her graves are round about him: all of them uncircumcised, slain by the sword, though they caused their terror in the land of the living [Ezek. 32:26].**

And Edom is there also—

> **There is Edom, her kings, and all her princes, which with their might are laid by them that were slain by the sword: they shall die with the uncircumcised, and with them that go down to the pit [Ezek. 32:29].**

Now listen to this—

> **For I have caused my terror in the land of the living: and he shall be laid in the midst of the uncircumcised with**

**them that are slain with the sword, even Pharaoh and
all his multitude, saith the Lord GOD [Ezek. 32:32].**

Ezekiel only gives us a glimpse of that unseen world called sheol.
Remember, we see only a fleeting view of this place. Don't try to build
a skyscraper, or a merchandise center, or a mall, or a shopping area,
on a place that only has a foundation big enough for a tool shed! In
other words, you can't build a theology on this, because all we have
had is a little peek into the unseen world. And it is all God intended
for us to see.

CHAPTER 33

THEME: Recommission of Ezekiel

Chapter 33 brings us to the last major division of this book. From chapters 33—48 we will see the glory of the Lord and the coming millennial Kingdom. Chapter 32 concluded the predictions concerning the nations that were round about Israel. Some of these nations were contiguous to the land of Israel. They were very closely related to them, of course—actually related by blood. These prophecies were given before the destruction of Jerusalem. Now we come to the second part of this prophetic book, which contains Ezekiel's prophecies *after* the fall of Jerusalem.

Ezekiel again is speaking of Jerusalem, and the land of Israel will be his subject, but his message is different. Up to chapter 25 everything pointed to the destruction of Jerusalem. Then Jerusalem was destroyed exactly as he had predicted. Now he will look forward to the future of the coming millennial Kingdom when the glory of the Lord will be seen again on this earth. That makes this a very interesting section.

Not only is Ezekiel's commission renewed, he will also be commended for the fact that he has done a good job up to this point. From now on he is going to be speaking to those in captivity, telling them that they are to live in the expectancy of the future. Before, these captives had no hope because of their sins. But in the future, Ezekiel sees hope for the children of Israel.

Today believers also have a hope. It is not anchored in anything that men do here on earth, or in any of the gyrations of psychoanalysis. Our hope today is not a philosophy. It rests upon the Word of God and what He has said will take place in the future. This is the lodestar of the child of God in our day. It is not the same as Israel moving into the Millennium. We are moving actually into the New Jerusalem. This is what is immediately ahead of us as believers.

RECOMMISSION OF THE PROPHET

Again the word of the Lord came unto me, saying [Ezek. 33:1].

This phrase is a stuck record as far as Ezekiel is concerned. He wants us to remember constantly that he is not giving us his theories or ideas, but he is giving out the Word of the Lord.

Son of man, speak to the children of thy people, and say unto them, When I bring the sword upon a land, if the people of the land take a man of their coasts, and set him for their watchman:

If when he seeth the sword come upon the land, he blow the trumpet, and warn the people [Ezek. 33:2–3].

God reverts to the commission that he gave to Ezekiel at the beginning of his ministry. He likens him to the watchman of a city. In that day most of the cities of importance were protected by walls. Those in authority appointed a watchman to watch for invaders from the top of the wall all during the hours of darkness. I imagine that during the night he would call off the watches with a shout of "All's well" when there was no moving of an approaching enemy out there in the darkness. The interesting thing is that the false prophets were saying "All's well" when the enemy was coming. They were too blind to see him. Ezekiel had been a faithful watchman and had given the people warning that the enemy, which was Babylon, was coming.

But if the watchman see the sword come, and blow not the trumpet, and the people be not warned; if the sword come, and take any person from among them, he is taken away in his iniquity; but his blood will I require at the watchman's hand [Ezek. 33:6].

Now the people are going to be judged for their sin, but the watchman will be held responsible if he doesn't warn them. Ezekiel had warned them; the false prophets had not. Ezekiel had done a good job.

> **So thou, O son of man, I have set thee a watchman unto the house of Israel; therefore thou shalt hear the word at my mouth, and warn them from me [Ezek. 33:7].**

Ezekiel has fulfilled that commission.

> **When I say unto the wicked, O wicked man, thou shalt surely die; if thou dost not speak to warn the wicked from his way, that wicked man shall die in his iniquity; but his blood will I require at thine hand [Ezek. 33:8].**

The responsibility of the watchman is to warn the wicked that they are going to be judged. Ezekiel was faithful in giving the warning, although the people would not listen to him. To sound the warning was the only way the watchman could clear himself.

Today the man who is teaching the Word of God is not required to get results. Many people say, "Let's get an evangelist who can get results." To get people to come forward in a meeting is not of primary importance. The preacher giving the people the Word of God is the important thing. I don't look at the folks who have come forward; I look at the people who walk out after the benediction. Have they been warned? That should be our concern. We have been looking at the wrong crowd. We say, "Oh, So-and-So gave such a sweet gospel invitation, and a lot of sweet people came forward. No decisions were actually made, but we had a movement going on." Oh, my friend, let's make sure that the fellow who hears has been properly warned. If he is not warned, the speaker is held responsible. He will have to answer to God for neglecting his duty.

> **Say unto them, As I live, saith the Lord God, I have no pleasure in the death of the wicked; but that the wicked turn from his way and live: turn ye, turn ye from your**

evil ways; for why will ye die, O house of Israel? [Ezek. 33:11].

It is quite obvious from this verse that God does not want to judge. Isaiah said that judgment was His *strange* work. God wants to save them, and He is urging them to turn to Him and accept life.

Yet the children of thy people say, The way of the Lord is not equal: but as for them, their way is not equal [Ezek. 33:17].

The children of Israel had another complaint. They said that God was not fair in His judgment. He judged everybody alike; yet there were some "good people" among the captives.

When the righteous turneth from his righteousness, and committeth iniquity, he shall even die thereby [Ezek. 33:18].

This verse is not speaking about somebody losing salvation. God is saying that when one of His children gets into sin, He will judge him. That is exactly what Paul said in 1 Corinthians 11:31: "For if we would judge ourselves, we should not be judged." And God says through John that there is a sin unto death (1 John 5:16). He is speaking about a child of God. What kind of death is he talking about? He is talking about physical death. Some Christians are judged for their sins by physical death. I am amazed that more folks don't catch on to God's discipline after a time. There are others who are in the Lord's work, but what they are doing is not prospering, and they are getting deeper and deeper into debt. You would think that the message would come through loud and clear that perhaps God is moving in judgment, that what they are doing is not pleasing to Him.

But if the wicked turn from his wickedness, and do that which is lawful and right, he shall live thereby [Ezek. 33:19].

God is righteous in what He does. If a wicked man will turn to God, God will save him.

Yet ye say, The way of the Lord is not equal. O ye house of Israel, I will judge you every one after his ways [Ezek. 33:20].

Godly men, too, were carried away into captivity. Those who had trusted God were carried off just like the most wicked people, and these godly people are complaining. It looks like God is being unfair.

You and I experience this same principle in many ways. For example, we have to pay excessive insurance premiums today because there are a lot of alcoholics. I don't drink, but I have to pay for the ones who do. I have to pay high taxes because we have a lot of folks in Washington today who spend money foolishly. We are identified with our nation.

And the good people in Israel were suffering because they were identified with the nation. But there is more to it than that. Notice what God says—

"O ye house of Israel, I will judge you every one after his ways." In other words, I am going to judge every one of you. And, my friend, whoever you are, you will have to stand before God for judgment some day. If you are a child of God, He will judge you for the sins you have committed, but you will not lose your salvation. However, if you are a lost person, you have no claim on God whatsoever. He has made that clear in the New Testament. In 1 Peter 3:12 we read, "For the eyes of the Lord are over the righteous, and his ears are open unto their prayers: but the face of the Lord is against them that do evil." God doesn't say that He won't hear the prayer of the wicked; He just says that He hears the prayers of the righteous, which implies that He feels no obligation to hear the prayer of the unsaved person. Of course, if he would cry out for salvation, God would hear and answer, but the point is that the unsaved person has no claim on God whatsoever. When you hear an unsaved person ask, "Why does God let this happen to me?" you know that he has no claim whatever on God's mercy. God is *righteous* when He is judging a lost world, and sometimes we forget that this happens to be *His* world.

THE CITY IS SMITTEN!

And it came to pass in the twelfth year of our captivity, in the tenth month, in the fifth day of the month, that one that had escaped out of Jerusalem came unto me, saying, The city is smitten [Ezek. 33:21].

Ezekiel had already said that Jerusalem was destroyed because God had told him, but as yet he had been given no information about it. When the news of the destruction of the city was brought to these people, it absolutely dumbfounded them. They were overwhelmed by the news. They never believed that anything like this could possibly take place. On the very day that this news was brought, Ezekiel's wife died, and God said to him in effect, "Don't grieve for your wife. I want these people to know that I have repudiated their city. They think that I have to have Jerusalem. They think that I won't destroy it. They don't believe I will judge sin, but I will. Therefore, don't weep for your wife. Let the people know that at this time the city is being destroyed because of its sin. The city is smitten."

Now the hand of the LORD was upon me in the evening, afore he that was escaped came; and had opened my mouth, until he came to me in the morning; and my mouth was opened, and I was no more dumb [Ezek. 33:22].

You see, at the end of chapter 24 God announced to Ezekiel the destruction of Jerusalem, the bloody city. From that point on (chs. 25—33) He had given him no prophecy for Jerusalem; instead, He had given him messages for the surrounding nations. Now when we come here to chapter 33, we find that God no longer makes Ezekiel dumb about

Jerusalem. He says to him, "I have some messages for you about Jerusalem now."

Then the word of the Lord came unto me, saying,

Son of man, they that inhabit those wastes of the land of Israel speak, saying, Abraham was one, and he inherited the land: but we are many; the land is given us for inheritance [Ezek. 33:23–24].

The people of Israel are remembering how God took care of Abraham; yet there was only one of him, and there are a whole lot of them. They expect Him to take care of them in the same way. They are ignoring the fact that there was a great deal of difference between Abraham and themselves. Abraham believed God, and it was counted to him for righteousness. These people do not believe God.

Wherefore say unto them, Thus saith the Lord God; Ye eat with the blood, and lift up your eyes toward your idols, and shed blood: and shall ye possess the land? [Ezek. 33:25].

God says to them, "I won't let you have the land. I put the heathen and the pagan out of this land because of their sin, and you are doing the same things they did."

For I will lay the land most desolate, and the pomp of her strength shall cease; and the mountains of Israel shall be desolate, that none shall pass through [Ezek. 33:28].

I cannot get as elated about the land of Israel as some of my very good minister friends do. When they get into that land, they go into ecstasy. The way some of them act you would think they were on drugs! They exclaim, "Isn't it wonderful to see this land!" I want to tell you that the land is just about as desolate as any place you could possibly find today. That land is desolate because the judgment of God is upon it.

There is a water shortage—put a little water on that land and it blossoms like a rose—but they can't get enough water. That is the great problem. God's judgment is not only upon a people; it is also upon a land.

> **Also, thou son of man, the children of thy people still are talking against thee by the walls and in the doors of the houses, and speak one to another, every one to his brother, saying, Come, I pray you, and hear what is the word that cometh forth from the LORD [Ezek. 33:30].**

The people are shaken, and they want to listen to Ezekiel now, but they won't follow through.

> **And they come unto thee as the people cometh, and they sit before thee as my people, and they hear thy words, but they will not do them: for with their mouth they shew much love, but their heart goeth after their covetousness [Ezek. 33:31].**

On the surface they appeared to be turning to the Lord. They wanted to hear what the Lord had to say but had no intention of obeying Him. They were like folk who go to church in our day to hear an interesting and well-delivered sermon, but what they hear does not change their lives. The Epistle of James gets down where the rubber meets the road when he says, "But be ye doers of the word, and not hearers only, deceiving your own selves" (James 1:22). This is what God says to Ezekiel about these folk in captivity, "They hear thy words, but they do them not."

> **And, lo, thou art unto them as a very lovely song of one that hath a pleasant voice, and can play well on an instrument: for they hear thy words, but they do them not.**

> **And when this cometh to pass, (lo, it will come,) then shall they know that a prophet hath been among them [Ezek. 33:32–33].**

Now that Jerusalem has fallen, as Ezekiel had prophesied, the people know he is a true prophet of God. Although they know he is giving them God's Word, they still will not obey it. My friend, unbelief is *willful*; it is not because mankind has a great mentality that cannot accept what God says. The real problem is that people do not want to give up their sin. That was the problem with the people to whom Ezekiel ministered. They were willing to come and listen to what Ezekiel had to say, but it had no effect upon them whatsoever. You would think that the people would now turn to God, but that was not the case. God said to Ezekiel, "Don't let the crowds deceive you. It is true that they are coming and listening, but they are not heeding what you say. They are not doers of the Word at all. They like it when they hear you talk about love, and the future, and prophecy, but it has not affected their lives one whit. They are still living the same way—far from Me."

Ezekiel was the *only* man who said that Jerusalem would be destroyed. All of the false prophets said that it would not be destroyed. The word of confirmation has come. Jerusalem is destroyed. Ezekiel is declared a true prophet.

CHAPTER 34

THEME: Israel's false shepherds; God's true shepherd

ISRAEL'S FALSE SHEPHERDS

The false prophets of Israel have now been shown to be liars because the destruction of Jerusalem as prophesied by Ezekiel has become a reality. God has a word to say about these false prophets:

And the word of the Lord came unto me, saying,

Son of man, prophesy against the shepherds of Israel, prophesy, and say unto them, Thus saith the Lord God unto the shepherds; Woe be to the shepherds of Israel that do feed themselves! should not the shepherds feed the flocks? [Ezek. 34:1–2].

Ezekiel did not say these things about the false prophets—God said them.

Very candidly, I have always been opposed to promotion—that is, furthering the growth or development of a Christian work. This does not mean that there aren't many very wonderful and fine works which deserve our financial support. My point is that they should not be just a promotion agency; they should be feeding the people—they should be giving out the Word of God. I feel that an organization has no right to fleece people for an offering when it has not given the people something first. We should be able to support ministries where we ourselves have received a blessing. The business of the ministry is not to beg for money all the time, but to give out the Word of God and to be feeding the sheep.

This was God's criticism of the false prophets—they had not given the people the Word of God. I feel this should still be the standard by which we judge a ministry today.

> **The diseased have ye not strengthened, neither have ye healed that which was sick, neither have ye bound up that which was broken, neither have ye brought again that which was driven away, neither have ye sought that which was lost; but with force and with cruelty have ye ruled them [Ezek. 34:4].**

All of us are needy people, and the only thing which can minister to our deep needs is the Word of God. If a minister is not giving the Word of God, he is not ministering to the people. The Word must be given out. These little sermonettes delivered to Christianettes by preacherettes are not quite doing the job today.

> **And they were scattered, because there is no shepherd: and they became meat to all the beasts of the field, when they were scattered [Ezek. 34:5].**

"Meat" could also be translated "food." In other words, when people are not being fed in a church, they will scatter. They'll go find some place where they can be fed. There is no point in criticizing them, because sheep want to be fed. That is also the nature of the child of God: he wants to hear the Word of God.

> **Therefore, ye shepherds, hear the word of the Lord;**
>
> **As I live, saith the Lord God, surely because my flock became a prey, and my flock became meat to every beast of the field, because there was no shepherd, neither did my shepherds search for my flock, but the shepherds fed themselves, and fed not my flock;**
>
> **Therefore, O ye shepherds, hear the word of the Lord;**
>
> **Thus saith the Lord God; Behold, I am against the shepherds; and I will require my flock at their hand, and cause them to cease from feeding the flock; neither shall the shepherds feed themselves any more; for I will de-**

liver my flock from their mouth, that they may not be meat for them [Ezek. 34:7–10].

God holds these false shepherds responsible. He says, "I am against them, and I am as much opposed to them as I am to any sinner or any sin. I'm going to hold them responsible."

GOD'S TRUE SHEPHERD

For thus saith the Lord GOD; Behold, I, even I, will both search my sheep, and seek them out [Ezek. 34:11].

Here you have God's Shepherd—Jesus, who said "I am the Good Shepherd." Ezekiel said that Christ would come, and, my friend, He is coming again because He has not yet fulfilled all the prophecies concerning His shepherding of this earth.

Now we begin to look into the future. These are God's words of comfort to the children of Israel in their captivity—they should listen to Him. He's the Shepherd, the Good Shepherd, the Great Shepherd, and the Chief Shepherd of the sheep. He says, "I will search out my sheep." David said, "The LORD is my shepherd; I shall not want" (Ps. 23:1).

The thing that impresses us in the rest of this chapter is the repetition of a wonderful statement by God, "I will," which occurs eighteen times in verses 11 through 29. I get a little weary listening to men speak of what they have done. This is a new note here—God says, "I will." This is grace when God says this. The Good Shepherd one day said, "Come unto me, all ye that labour and are heavy laden, and I *will* give you rest [rest you]" (Matt. 11:28, italics mine). The Shepherd also said, "I [*will*] give unto them eternal life; and they shall never perish . . ." (John 10:28). That is what my wonderful Shepherd said.

As a shepherd seeketh out his flock in the day that he is among his sheep that are scattered; so will I seek out my sheep, and will deliver them out of all places where they

have been scattered in the cloudy and dark day [Ezek. 34:12].

The Good Shepherd came more than nineteen hundred years ago, and He still says, "My sheep hear my voice . . ." (John 10:27). Do you know why they hear His voice? There are two reasons: He is *calling* them, and His sheep *know* Him. They hear His voice, and they know Him. What a wonderful Shepherd we have!

And I will bring them out from the people, and gather them from the countries, and will bring them to their own land, and feed them upon the mountains of Israel by the rivers, and in all the inhabited places of the country [Ezek. 34:13].

The Shepherd is talking about the nation of Israel, what He is going to do for them in the future. They are in captivity now because of their sin and because they listened to the false prophets. But He says, "I am not through with them. I have not thrown them overboard. You amillennialists ought to read the Book of Ezekiel; then you would find out that I am not through with My sheep—I intend to bring them back to their land."

I will feed them in a good pasture, and upon the high mountains of Israel shall their fold be: there shall they lie in a good fold, and in a fat pasture shall they feed upon the mountains of Israel.

I will feed my flock, and I will cause them to lie down, saith the Lord GOD [Ezek. 34:14–15].

He will feed them in a good pasture, and when they lie down they will be safe. Obviously this is for a future time. The land of Israel does not lie in safety at all today.

I will seek that which was lost, and bring again that which was driven away, and will bind up that which

was broken, and will strengthen that which was sick: but I will destroy the fat and the strong; I will feed them with judgment [Ezek. 34:16].

When He has one lost sheep, this Shepherd goes out to find it. He will do that for the nation Israel, and He will do that for the church today. When our Lord told the parable of the lost sheep, that shepherd had one hundred sheep, and one sheep got lost. What did the shepherd do? Did he just forget about that sheep? Did he say, "Well, if one little one wants to run off, that's all right; after all, ninety-nine sheep is a pretty good number to come through with"? No, this shepherd said, "I started out with one hundred and I am going to come through with one hundred." My friend, Vernon McGee is going to be in heaven—not because he's a smart sheep; all sheep are stupid—I am going to be there because I've got a wonderful Shepherd, and He says, "I will, I will," again and again.

Therefore thus saith the Lord God unto them; Behold, I, even I, will judge between the fat cattle and between the lean cattle [Ezek. 34:20].

God is going to do the separating. In Matthew 13, the Lord Jesus gave the parable of the tares among the wheat. He told of a man who sowed good seed in his field, but an enemy came in and sowed tares among the good seed. The man's servant said, "Let's go pull up the tares," but the man said, "You let them alone; let the wheat and the tares grow together. I'll do the separating." I am glad that the separating is the Lord's job. That is His business. When someone comes to me and says, "Do you think So-and-So is a believer?" I have to say that I don't know. That's not my business; that's the Lord's business. He knows the ones who are His.

Because ye have thrust with side and with shoulder, and pushed all the diseased with your horns, till ye have scattered them abroad;

Therefore will I save my flock, and they shall no more be a prey; and I will judge between cattle and cattle.

And I will set up one shepherd over them, and he shall feed them, even my servant David; he shall feed them, and he shall be their shepherd.

And I the LORD will be their God, and my servant David a prince among them; I the LORD have spoken it [Ezek. 34:21-24].

It is my firm conviction that the earth will be the eternal home of Israel and that David will rule here on this earth throughout eternity. He will be vice-regent of the Lord Jesus. I believe the church will be in the New Jerusalem with the Lord—the Lord Jesus said that He was coming again to take the church, ". . . that where I am, there ye may be also" (John 14:3). And throughout eternity when He comes to earth, we will come also, but just for a visit. Therefore, don't buy too much real estate down here—you won't be needing it—but be sure you are sending up plenty of material to build a good home in heaven!

"I the LORD have spoken it." My friend, He says He is not through with the nation Israel.

And I will make with them a covenant of peace, and will cause the evil beasts to cease out of the land: and they shall dwell safely in the wilderness, and sleep in the woods [Ezek. 34:25].

It is quite interesting that the land and the people of Israel go together in Scripture. When they are in the land and being blessed, that means that the people are in a right relationship to God.

And they shall no more be a prey to the heathen, neither shall the beast of the land devour them; but they shall

dwell safely, and none shall make them afraid [Ezek. 34:28].

The day will come when Israel will "no more be a prey to the heathen [the nations]." They are still that today, but God says, "I will," and when He says that, He *is* going to do it, my friend.

CHAPTERS 35 AND 36

THEME: Edom judged; prediction of Israel's sins judged and forgiven

Chapters 35 and 36 deal with the future restoration of Israel. There are two things which must happen before the people can be restored to the land in peace: Edom must be judged, and Israel's past sins must be judged and forgiven. The judgment predicted here was fulfilled upon Edom, but it also is prophetic of the judgment which is in store for the enemies of Israel which is still future in our day.

EDOM JUDGED

Chapter 35 deals with the judgment and removal of Mount Seir (or Edom) which must take place before Israel can be restored to the land.

> Moreover the word of the Lord came unto me, saying,
>
> Son of man, set thy face against mount Seir, and prophesy against it,
>
> And say unto it, Thus saith the Lord God; Behold, O mount Seir, I am against thee, and I will stretch out mine hand against thee, and I will make thee most desolate.
>
> I will lay thy cities waste, and thou shalt be desolate, and thou shalt know that I am the Lord [Ezek. 35:1–4].

These verses refer to Edom, and in Edom there was the rock-hewn city known as Petra. The city is still there, but there is no more desolate area anywhere than that place.

> Because thou hast had a perpetual hatred, and hast shed the blood of the children of Israel by the force of the

sword in the time of their calamity, in the time that their iniquity had an end [Ezek. 35:5].

God gives the reason for the judgment of Edom. Edom is the people descended from Esau, Jacob's brother. Esau was Jacob's bitterest enemy, and the people of Edom probably hurt the people of Israel more than any other enemy they had. Edom represents the enemy of God in this world today, that enemy who is going to rise against God in the last days under the Antichrist.

I will make thee perpetual desolations, and thy cities shall not return: and ye shall know that I am the LORD [Ezek. 35:9].

Ezekiel has previously mentioned Edom's judgment in Ezekiel 25:12–14. Why does he mention it here again? I believe that it is to show that God has a program for the nation Israel. They are to be restored to the land, a place of blessing. They will be put back in the land in peace. However, the enemy is still about, and so God will judge the enemy. The people will be back in the land worshiping God, and living in peace and blessing. What a glorious future is ahead for them!

ISRAEL'S PAST SINS JUDGED AND FORGIVEN

In chapter 36 we find that Israel's past sins must be judged and forgiven before she can be restored to the land.

Therefore thus saith the LORD GOD; Surely in the fire of my jealousy have I spoken against the residue of the heathen, and against all Idumea, which have appointed my land into their possession with the joy of all their heart, with despiteful minds, to cast it out for a prey [Ezek. 36:5].

God is determined that the wicked will not inherit the earth. He has made it clear: ". . . the meek . . . shall inherit the earth" (Matt. 5:5).

The meek are not inheriting it today. The wicked are the ones who have it, and they are the ones who are prospering.

This chapter contains the prophecy concerning the fact that the land of Israel is to be restored. All you have to do is drive through that land, and you will know this prophecy is not yet fulfilled. A great many people like to think they see prophecy being fulfilled on every hand, but when God brings them back to the land, the land is to be blessed. It is not blessed today, my friend.

> **Prophesy therefore concerning the land of Israel, and say unto the mountains, and to the hills, to the rivers, and to the valleys, Thus saith the Lord God; Behold, I have spoken in my jealousy and in my fury, because ye have borne the shame of the heathen:**

> **Therefore thus saith the Lord God; I have lifted up mine hand, Surely the heathen that are about you, they shall bear their shame.**

> **But ye, O mountains of Israel, ye shall shoot forth your branches, and yield your fruit to my people of Israel; for they are at hand to come [Ezek. 36:6–8].**

"For they are at hand to come" could be translated "For they are soon to come." "Soon" to God is different from what it is to us; after all, a day is as a thousand years with Him.

> **Moreover the word of the LORD came unto me, saying,**

> **Son of man, when the house of Israel dwelt in their own land, they defiled it by their own way and by their doings: their way was before me as the uncleanness of a removed woman.**

> **Wherefore I poured my fury upon them for the blood that they had shed upon the land, and for their idols wherewith they had polluted it [Ezek. 36:16–18].**

Again may I emphasize that the land and the people belong together. The Mosaic Law was not only given to a people, it was given for a land.

> **And I scattered them among the heathen, and they were dispersed through the countries: according to their way and according to their doings I judged them [Ezek. 36:19].**

God says, "I scattered them among the heathen [the nations]," but listen to Him:

> **But I had pity for mine holy name, which the house of Israel had profaned among the heathen, whither they went.**

> **Therefore say unto the house of Israel, Thus saith the Lord GOD; I do not this for your sakes, O house of Israel, but for mine holy name's sake, which ye have profaned among the heathen, whither ye went.**

> **And I will sanctify my great name, which was profaned among the heathen, which ye have profaned in the midst of them; and the heathen shall know that I am the LORD, saith the Lord GOD, when I shall be sanctified in you before their eyes [Ezek. 36:21–23].**

You see, God has yet to defend His name in this earth. There are a great many people who ridicule the church today and the people who are in it. They blaspheme God because of it. God is going to justify Himself in this earth, and He is going to sanctify His name down here. Many take His name in vain today, but God says, "That's going to stop, and you are going to honor Me." This is *His* world, you see.

> **A new heart also will I give you, and a new spirit will I put within you: and I will take away the stony heart out**

of your flesh, and I will give you an heart of flesh [Ezek. 36:26].

God says what He is going to do. A change is going to take place. "A new heart also will I give you"—they are going to be born again.

And I will put my spirit within you, and cause you to walk in my statutes, and ye shall keep my judgments, and do them [Ezek. 36:27].

This is what Joel meant in his prophecy—there is a day coming when God will pour out His Spirit on all flesh, not just *some*. The Spirit was poured out upon very few on the Day of Pentecost. All Peter said on that day was, "Don't ridicule us and say we are drunk. This is *like* what Joel said is going to happen in the last days." The Spirit has come upon a few, and today God is calling out a people for His name. The minute you turn to Christ, you are regenerated by the Holy Spirit; you are indwelt and baptized by the Holy Spirit; you are put in the body of believers. "In that day," God says, "I'll put My Spirit within you."

And ye shall dwell in the land that I gave to your fathers; and ye shall be my people, and I will be your God.

I will also save you from all your uncleanness: and I will call for the corn, and will increase it, and lay no famine upon you [Ezek. 36:28–29].

They will dwell in the land, and there will be prosperity in the land. God has promised to them *physical* blessings, just as He has promised to us *spiritual* blessings.

This chapter concludes with a great prophecy:

And they shall say, This land that was desolate is become like the garden of Eden; and the waste and desolate and ruined cities are become fenced, and are inhabited.

Then the heathen that are left round about you shall know that I the LORD build the ruined places, and plant that that was desolate: I the LORD have spoken it, and I will do it.

Thus saith the Lord GOD; I will yet for this be inquired of by the house of Israel, to do it for them; I will increase them with men like a flock.

As the holy flock, as the flock of Jerusalem in her solemn feasts; so shall the waste cities be filled with flocks of men: and they shall know that I am the Lord [Ezek. 36:35–38].

"And they shall say, This land that was desolate is become like the garden of Eden." You can say that if you want to, but it wouldn't be true today.

"And they shall know that I am the LORD." They don't know that in Israel, they don't know it in the United States, and they don't know it in the world today. But the day is coming, my friend, when Israel will know that He is the Lord.

CHAPTER 37

THEME: Vision of the valley of dead bones, picturing the Resurrection of Israel

THE VISION OF THE VALLEY OF DEAD BONES

In this chapter we have the vision of the valley of dead bones which served as the basis for a Negro spiritual written some years ago, entitled, "Dem Bones." The interpretation of this chapter concerns the future restoration of Israel. That restoration has to do both with the *national* entity of Israel as well as the *spiritual* revival or restoration which the Lord announced in the preceding chapter.

We have here a remarkable vision, and I would like to make it very clear that this vision does *not* have to do with the resurrection of the dead saints of the church. That is the giant leap in interpretation made by the many who spiritualize the prophetic section of the Old Testament. My friend, when we take prophecy *literally*, it will make sense. We are talking here about the nation Israel, and we are not talking about a spiritual or physical resurrection of individuals. In my notes I have labeled this chapter, "The Resurrection of Israel," and I think that is a good title, but it is sometimes misunderstood. Some think that I am referring to the raising of the dead from Abraham on. It has no reference to that, but it definitely refers to the *nation* of Israel.

God gives to Ezekiel a real living parable and to do so He takes him to the valley of dead bones:

> **The hand of the LORD was upon me, and carried me out in the spirit of the LORD, and set me down in the midst of the valley which was full of bones [Ezek. 37:1].**

Before Jerusalem was destroyed by Nebuchadnezzar, Ezekiel was transported to Jerusalem (see ch. 8), and I do not believe God had any difficulty doing that. If man today can make a jet plane which can carry him halfway around the world in half a day, I see no reason why

God cannot do something which is commensurate with who He is. So I don't think that God had any difficulty getting Ezekiel up and taking him to Jerusalem.

Here again, I believe God literally moves Ezekiel. When Ezekiel says that He "carried me out in the spirit of the LORD," he is saying that the Spirit of the Lord carried him out to the valley which was full of bones.

> **And caused me to pass by them round about: and, behold, there were very many in the open valley; and, lo, they were very dry [Ezek. 37:2].**

Back in 1849, Lewis Manly and his partner by the name of John Rogers crossed Death Valley in California to bring back supplies to the stranded Bennett-Arcane party. The Bennett-Arcane group had mistakenly wandered into Death Valley and would have perished if these two men had not crossed the valley to rescue them. They were actually the first white men to cross this valley and gaze upon its grand scene of death and desolation. Few men have seen such sights, but what Ezekiel saw some twenty-five hundred years earlier must have been even more bleak. He saw a vision of another "death valley," more desolate, more fearsome, and more awesome than Death Valley, California.

The valley which Ezekiel saw was filled with dead bones, and the thing which characterized them is that they were very dry and they were scattered.

> **And he said unto me, Son of man, can these bones live? And I answered, O Lord GOD, thou knowest [Ezek. 37:3].**

These bones scattered all over the place are human bones, and the question that is put to Ezekiel is, "Can these bones live?" Ezekiel answers, "O Lord GOD, thou knowest." In other words, he said, "I don't see how they could. It's beyond me—You alone know whether these dead bones can live or not!"

Again he said unto me, Prophesy upon these bones, and say unto them, O ye dry bones, hear the word of the LORD [Ezek. 37:4].

This is something rather ironical and even humorous. I have always insisted that God has a sense of humor, and here is an illustration of that. If you can't see where it's funny, that's all right—just pass it by. But imagine Ezekiel now as God says to him, "Prophesy on these bones. Start out by saying, 'O ye dry bones, hear the word of the LORD.'" I have a notion Ezekiel said, "Now, Lord, you really don't mean for me to start *talking* to these dry bones here! The man with the white coat and the net will be out looking for me if I do that!" Really, that isn't a very good sermon introduction is it? No preacher would begin by saying to his Sunday morning congregation, "Oh, you dry bones!" A friend of mine (who also has a good sense of humor) said to me, "You know, I have a congregation with which I'd like to begin as Ezekiel did—the bones I speak to are as dry as Ezekiel's—but I don't dare do that."

Ezekiel is looking out on this valley filled with dry bones, and he's to speak to them. Every congregation that a preacher speaks to includes those who are saved and those who are unsaved. Those who are saved may have ears to hear, but do not hear. And the ones who are not saved are dead in trespasses and sins—they haven't been redeemed yet. The preacher is just as helpless as Ezekiel, for any preacher who understands the real state and condition of those who are lost recognizes his own helplessness in speaking to them. Ezekiel is to say to these bones, "I want you to hear what God has to say."

Thus saith the Lord GOD unto these bones, Behold I will cause breath to enter into you, and ye shall live.

And I will lay sinews upon you, and will bring up flesh upon you, and cover you with skin, and put breath in you, and ye shall live; and ye shall know that I am the LORD [Ezek. 37:5–6].

God says, "I want you to speak to them and tell them I'll be the One who will give them life." That is our condition today—if God doesn't move, no one has spiritual life. I receive letters from people who say, "You saved me." My friend, I save no one. I just speak to dry bones, giving them the Word of God—that's all I do. The Spirit of God is the One who has to bring life. That is the only way life can come. This is the *application* of these verses; we are going to see that they also have a tremendous *interpretation*.

So I prophesied as I was commanded: and as I prophesied, there was a noise, and behold a shaking, and the bones came together, bone to his bone [Ezek. 37:7].

"So I prophesied as I was commanded"—this man Ezekiel obeys God.

"There was a noise, and behold a shaking, and the bones came together, bone to his bone." This is the point where that Negro spiritual, "Dem Bones," is really accurate—when the bones start coming together. I'm of the opinion Ezekiel had a rather funny feeling when in his vision he saw all these bones come together!

And when I beheld, lo, the sinews and the flesh came up upon them, and the skin covered them above: but there was no breath in them [Ezek. 37:8].

We have here a method which I want you to notice. The first state of the bones is that they are scattered, dry, and dead. Then gradually they come together, and the sinews and flesh come upon them. This is a process—it is not instantaneous at all. At this point in the vision all you have is a bunch of bodies, actually corpses; it is just an undertaking establishment down in that valley. They are no longer bones, but bodies with flesh upon them. They are human beings even, but they do not have any life in them.

Then said he unto me, Prophesy unto the wind, prophesy, son of man, and say to the wind, Thus saith the

> Lord GOD; Come from the four winds, O breath, and
> breathe upon these slain, that they may live.
>
> So I prophesied as he commanded me, and the breath
> came into them, and they lived, and stood up upon their
> feet, an exceeding great army [Ezek. 37:9–10].

Ezekiel spoke, and life came into those bodies. What happened here
resembles the creation of man at the very beginning. God took man of
the dust of the earth; Ezekiel started with bones, but God didn't. God
started with just the dirt of the earth, and then He breathed life into
man.

Now what has happened to these bones has occurred in three
stages: (1) they were scattered bones, just as dead as they could be; (2)
then they came together, and flesh and skin came upon them—they
were bodies, but *dead* bodies; and finally (3) they were made alive. We
will find in these three stages a real key to understanding Bible prophecy concerning the nation Israel.

Now this verse explains the meaning of the vision:

> Then he said unto me, Son of man, these bones are the
> whole house of Israel: behold, they say, Our bones are
> dried, and our hope is lost: we are cut off for our parts
> [Ezek. 37:11].

"Son of man, these bones are the whole house of Israel." We are not
talking here about the church; we are talking about *the house of Israel*.

"Behold, they say, Our bones are dried, and our hope is lost: we
are cut off for our parts." You see, the people in captivity had gone
from one extreme to another. As long as Jerusalem had stood and the
false prophets continued to say they would return, they maintained a
false hope. Now that Jerusalem has been destroyed, they go to the
other extreme—they have what psychologists call manic depressive
psychosis. They are in a bad state: they were high up one day, but now
they have hit the very depths. They say, "We have no hope." This vision is being given to them to let them know they do have a hope, and
it is for the whole house of Israel.

> Therefore prophesy and say unto them, Thus saith the Lord GOD; Behold, O my people, I will open your graves, and cause you to come up out of your graves, and bring you into the land of Israel [Ezek. 37:12].

After reading this verse, someone is apt to say, "Wait a minute. You said this vision was not concerning physical resurrection." I still insist upon that. Let's drop down to verse 21:

> And say unto them, Thus saith the Lord GOD; Behold, I will take the children of Israel from among the heathen, whither they be gone, and will gather them on every side, and bring them into their own land [Ezek. 37:21].

This is what God meant in verse 12 when He said, "I will cause you to come up out of your graves." Israel is buried in the nations of the world, and they are to be brought back and become a nation again.

I want to say something very carefully now concerning the three stages of the bones Ezekiel saw. I have said they are the key to understanding the future of the nation Israel, and I now want to add that if there is any place we have fulfilled prophecy, it is in these three stages. I don't go much for finding prophecy being fulfilled on every hand, but I do see it here. Follow me carefully: The nation Israel was buried and scattered in the nations of the world, and was dead to God, dead to the things of God—that's the first stage of the bones that we saw. Now since 1948 they have come back as a nation, but it is really a corpse over there today. They have a flag, they have a constitution, they have a prime minister, and they have a parliament. They have a police force and an army. They have a nation, and they even have Jerusalem. They have everything except spiritual life. If you walk from the old Arab section of Jerusalem where Islam dominates and come over into the Israeli section, there is no spiritual life. I want to say this kindly, but, as far as I am concerned, there is as much spiritual deadness on the one side as the other. There is a great deal more of that which is materialistic, which is intellectual, and which denotes civilization on the Israeli side, but there is no spiritual life whatsoever.

This is symbolized by the second stage of the bones—bodies, but without life. That is where Israel stands today.

In verses 15–28 Ezekiel mentions two sticks. I will not go into any detail here other than to say that they typify the northern (Israel) and southern (Judah) kingdoms which will again become one nation. This means, my friend, that there must not be any "ten lost tribes of Israel"—at least, if there are, God knows where they are, and I am confident that it is not Great Britain which will be joined to them in that land!

> **And I will make them one nation in the land upon the mountains of Israel; and one king shall be king to them all: and they shall be no more two nations, neither shall they be divided into two kingdoms any more at all [Ezek. 37:22].**

God will make them one nation.

> **And David my servant shall be king over them; and they all shall have one shepherd: they shall also walk in my judgments, and observe my statutes, and do them [Ezek. 37:24].**

That one Shepherd is none other than the Lord Jesus Christ. When He came, He was born in the line of David. Read Matthew 1; Luke 1 and 2—both very carefully record that He came in the line of David. The One that came in that line is the Shepherd, and He will rule over them. I personally believe that God will raise up David to reign over Israel, either in the Millennium or in the eternal Kingdom which will be ushered in immediately following the Millennium. Some commentators say he will reign in the Millennium; others say it will be the eternal Kingdom. I believe he will reign during both, that he will serve as the vice-regent of the Lord Jesus Christ down here on this earth.

And the heathen shall know that I the LORD do sanctify Israel, when my sanctuary shall be in the midst of them for evermore [Ezek. 37:28].

This is going to come to pass—it has not yet come to pass.

"When my sanctuary shall be in the midst of them for evermore." There will be a millennial temple for an eternal temple down here on the earth. In Revelation where it speaks of there not being a temple, it is referring to the New Jerusalem, which is where the church will be and which is not to be upon this earth. The eternal home of the children of Israel will be upon this earth, and God's temple will be in their midst. Although there is no doubt that Israel is the subject of Ezekiel, and especially of chapters 37—39, we can certainly make an application of it for our personal lives. The world that you and I live in today is a death valley, full of dead bones, dead people, if you please. Oh, people talk about being alive and say they are where the action is, but they are really dead in trespasses and sins. They have no spiritual life. That is the reason they have to have a drink or two, or take some sort of drugs, or do something to liven up the old corpse.

God has made it very clear that "He that hath the Son hath life; and he that hath not the Son of God hath not life" (1 John 5:12). If you have the Son of God, you have life. If you do not have the Son, you are dead. There are two kinds of people: live people and dead people. "He that believeth on the Son hath everlasting life: and he that believeth not the Son shall not see life; but the wrath of God abideth on him" (John 3:36). That means that the person without the Son is dead.

God is saying to you today that you are dead if you are not a Christian. Ye dry bones, hear the Word of the Lord. You can come to life. Accept Jesus Christ as your Savior. This is the application we can draw from this portion of Scripture, but the subject of the prophecy is the nation Israel.

CHAPTERS 38 AND 39

THEME: Russia's (Gog's) invasion of Israel

If there is any section in the prophecy of Ezekiel that is familiar, it is chapters 38 and 39. These two chapters tell of the repudiation of Gog and Magog. I am going to attempt to handle these chapters just a little differently than I generally do because I am anxious to lift out certain great truths for our consideration. Unfortunately, these chapters have been interpreted by men who apparently have no knowledge of the prophecy of Ezekiel and what goes with it. As a result they have come up with some very odd interpretations. They remind me of the advertisement that was put in the *Mines Magazine* in El Paso, Texas, by some fellows who were mining experts and engineers. They put an ad in that magazine in a deadpan way, as though it was serious. "Wanted: Man to work on nuclear fissionable isotopes, molecular reactive counters and three-phased cyclotronic uranium photosynthesizers. No experience necessary." Well, it is equally as humorous to try to interpret Ezekiel without knowing what the entire book is about.

We saw in chapter 37 that God has a definite purpose for Israel in the future, and these two chapters deal with that subject. They tell about the final enemy that will come against Israel in the last days.

In chapters 38 and 39 I believe that the enemy mentioned is Russia. When I entered the ministry, I did not believe that it referred to Russia. I refused to accept that interpretation because I had attended my denominational seminary which taught amillennialism. They did not believe that Russia was being referred to in this portion of Scripture. Even after I had worked for my doctoral degree, even at the time of my graduation, I still had not accepted it. Finally I came to the conclusion that I had better study the subject on my own, and I am convinced that the enemy of chapters 38 and 39 is Russia. Three points of contact make me know this in my own heart and mind: You have here what is known as the linguistic phenomenon, the geographic phenomenon, and the philosophical or idealogical phenomenon.

LINGUISTIC PHENOMENON

And the word of the LORD came unto me, saying,

Son of man, set thy face against Gog, the land of Magog, the chief prince of Meshech and Tubal, and prophesy against him [Ezek. 38:1–2].

Gog is a word for ruler, meaning roof, which actually means "the man on top." I can't think of a better name for a dictator than Gog. If he is not on top, he is not a dictator, and if he is on top, he is a dictator.

Magog means "head"; it is the Hebrew word *Rosh*, which means head. Dean Stanley, in his exhaustive *History of the Eastern Church*, published half a century ago, has a note founded on Gesenius, the great Hebrew scholar, to the effect that the word *Rosh* should be *Russia*. Then Dean Stanley adds that this is the only reference to a modern nation in the entire Old Testament. This is indeed remarkable.

Bishop Lowther made the statement that *Rosh* taken as a proper name in Ezekiel signified the inhabitants of Scythia from whom the modern Russians derive their name. You see, Russia was first called Muscovy, derived from Meshech. Ivan the Fourth, a czar of Russia, who was called Ivan the Terrible, came to the Muscovite throne in 1533. He assumed the title of Czar, which was the first time the title was used. I am sure you detect that the names Meshech and Tubal certainly sound like Moscow, and Tobolsk, which is way over in Siberia. The linguistic phenomenon certainly leads us to believe that Ezekiel is talking about Russia in this passage.

GEOGRAPHIC PHENOMENON

Now the second proof that identifies Russia is the geographic position. Here we have mentioned the nations which will be with Russia in the last days: "Gomer, and all his bands: the house of Togarmah of the north quarters, and all his bands: and many people with thee" (v. 6). "Gomer" is Germany, and "the house of Togarmah" is Turkey. "Of the north quarters" gives us the geographic location. Again in verse 15 we read: "And thou shalt come from thy place out of the north parts," and in chapter 39 verse 2 the same location is given: "and will cause thee to come up from the north parts." Whenever I give an illustrated message on this passage in Scripture, I always show a map of Israel and Russia. The literal meaning here is the "uttermost parts of the north." If you look at a map, you will find that Russia is directly north and northeast. In fact, it covers Israel just like that picture you have seen of the fellow under a great big sombrero. That hat covers him just like Russia covers the nation Israel. When you start going north of Israel, you end up in Russia, and when you get through Russia you will be among the icebergs. You and the polar bears are going to be the only ones there.

Directions in the Bible are in relation to the land of Israel. North in the Bible does not mean north of California or north of where you live. In the Bible north is north of the land of Israel. South is south of the land of Israel. West is west of the land of Israel, and east is east of the land of Israel. In other words, Israel is the geographical center of the earth as far as the Word of God is concerned.

PHILOSOPHICAL PHENOMENON

Finally we come to the philosophical or ideological phenomenon which helps us identify Gog and Magog with Russia.

> **And say, Thus saith the Lord God; Behold, I am against thee, O Gog, the chief prince of Meshech and Tubal [Ezek. 38:3].**

This is strange language. Here in the Book of Ezekiel God has said several times that He is against certain nations. He said it about Babylon; He said it about Egypt; and He said it about the nations which were against His people and against His person. Now here is a nation that is to arise in the last days, a nation which is against God. The reason we know it is against God is because God says, "I'm against you." This makes it different from any other nation, because God has said this about nations already in existence that have exhibited enmity and rejection of Him, but this nation hadn't even come into existence when Ezekiel gave this prophecy. Yet God says He is against it.

My friend, you and I have seen something that no generation in the past has seen. We have seen a nation arise whose basic philosophy is atheism. The political economy of Russia rests upon the premise that there is no God. It is atheistic. No other nation has assumed the dominant position of atheism.

Someone may be thinking, "What about the heathen, pagan nations of the past? Weren't they atheistic?" No, they were not. They were polytheistic. They believed in many gods. In the beginning men went off the track, but they did not become atheists. The reason they did not become atheists is, I think, easy to understand. They were too close to the mooring mast of revelation. After all, in Noah's day you did not have atheists. That was not the problem with that crowd at all. The problem with them was that they had gone off into sin, and they worshiped many gods. Man at that point was polytheistic. All the great nations of the past were polytheistic, and the judgments God has pronounced in this book are against polytheistic nations. He said of Memphis that all of the idols would disappear, and they have disappeared. There were probably no people so given over to idolatry—with the possible exception of the Babylonians. Polytheism characterized the ancient world. But Russia is a nation whose basic philosophy is atheistic, a nation that is against God.

Do you realize that God did not give a commandment against atheism at the beginning? He did, however, give the first two commandments against polytheism: "Thou shalt have no other gods before me" (Exod. 20:3); and "Thou shalt not make unto thee any graven image, or any likeness of any thing that is in heaven above, or that is in the earth beneath, or that is in the water under the earth" (Exod. 20:4). So, you see, there are commandments against polytheism, but none against atheism.

When you reach the time of David, atheism is beginning to appear. In Psalm 14:1 we read, "The fool hath said in his heart, There is no God." How ridiculous atheism is! It is almost an untenable position for little man, and here is a *nation* that says there is no God! Concerning Russia, men in high places have warned, "You cannot negotiate with them." Mr. Churchill said of Russia, "A riddle wrapped in a mystery inside an enigma." Rube Goldberg, who drew one of those crazy cartoons years ago, called Joe Stalin, "The Great Upside-down Philosopher." Underneath the cartoon was written: "Top is bottom, black is white, far is near, and day is night. Big is little, high is low, cold is hot, and yes is no." Unreasonable? Insane? But that has been the basic philosophy of Russia, and it is a nation that has risen in our day.

Mr. Stalin once said, "We have deposed the czars of the earth, and we shall now dethrone the Lord of heaven." When Russia put a rocket past the moon, called the *Sputnik*, and when it was nearing the sun, the following was heard on the radio in Russia: "Our rocket has bypassed the moon. It is nearing the sun. We have not discovered God. We have turned out lights in heaven that no man will be able to put on again. We are breaking the yoke of the gospel, the opiate of the masses. Let us go forth and Christ shall be relegated to mythology." I have often wondered what they had in mind when they said that. Did they think that God was playing peekaboo on the other side of the moon? Because they got a glimpse of the other side of the moon and did not see God, did that prove He did not exist? That is the reasoning of the upside-down philosopher. God, however, has beaten them to the draw. Before Russia even came into existence, God said, "I am against thee."

You can see how Gog and Magog may be identified with Russia by this threefold reason: (1) the linguistic phenomenon; (2) the geographic phenomenon; and (3) the philosophical or ideological phenonemon. These are the three points of identification, and when we get to chapter 39 of Ezekiel, God repeats once again that He is against Russia.

This chapter will tell us that this nation in the north with other nations with him will come down against Israel.

WHY RUSSIA WILL INVADE ISRAEL

Now the question is: Why will they come against the land of Israel?

And I will turn thee back, and put hooks into thy jaws, and I will bring thee forth, and all thine army, horses and horsemen, all of them clothed with all sorts of armour, even a great company with bucklers and shields, all of them handling swords [Ezek. 38:4].

God says, "I will . . . put hooks into thy jaws, and I will bring thee forth." This has been interpreted to mean that God was going to put hooks in their jaws to get them *out* of Israel after they had invaded it. But that is not what He says. He makes it clear that He is going to judge them *in* the land of Israel, and that they will not come out alive. In chapter 39, verse 11, He says, "And it shall come to pass in that day, that I will give unto Gog a place there of *graves in Israel*." As we read this section, it becomes obvious that God is not going to lead out the invading nations, but there will be a slaughter the like of which probably has not been seen in the history of the world.

Then what does God mean by saying that He will put hooks in their jaws? Well, it seems obvious to me that He is saying, "I am going to put hooks in your jaws and bring you down into the land of Israel." When this time comes, Israel will be back in their own land. For centuries that land was not occupied by them. After the destruction by Titus the Roman in A.D. 70, the Jewish people were sold into slavery throughout the world, and they were scattered throughout the world.

The land was no longer a land of milk and honey. We have seen in the Book of Ezekiel that even the Negev was at one time covered with forest. God said that He was going to burn that out, and He did. That is the place where Elijah went when Jezebel threatened to kill him. He kept going until he was so tired he stopped and crawled under a juniper tree. If Elijah were here today, he would have trouble finding a juniper tree to crawl under; he would have to find something else. The forests are gone.

Mark Twain said concerning the land of Israel, "Palestine sits in sackcloth and ashes, desolate and unlovely. It is a hopeless, dreary, heartbroken land. And why should it be otherwise? Can the curse of the Deity beautify a land? Palestine is no more of this work-day world. It is sacred to poetry and tradition. It is dreamland."

Dr. Theodor Herzl, the playwright from Austria who began the tremendous Zionist movement back to the land of Palestine, made this statement: "There is a land without a people. There is a people without a land. Give that land without a people to the people without a land."

Dr. Chaim Weizmann, the first president of Israel, speaking before the Anglo-American Commission of Inquiry, said, "The Jewish nation is a ghost nation. Only the God of Israel has kept the Jewish people alive."

David Ben-Gurion, the first prime minister and minister of defense in Israel, made this statement: "Ezekiel 37 has been fulfilled, and the nation Israel is hearing the footsteps of the Messiah."

Today Israel has turned from this thinking. I have a picture, taken on Israel's twenty-first anniversary, of a motto in the auditorium at Tel Aviv, written in Hebrew and English. It said, "Science will bring peace to this land." The Old Testament says that Messiah will bring peace to that land, so apparently they are chasing a new messiah today.

Russia will invade the land of Israel. Lord Beverly made the statement that Russia would not move into western Europe but would move into Asia and the Near East. General Douglas MacArthur concurred with him in that viewpoint. At the time Lord Beverly made that statement almost everyone thought that Russia would move into western Europe after World War II, but they did not move into that area at all. In fact, up to this day they have not moved into that area.

God says, "I will put hooks into thy jaws, and I will bring thee forth." Today I believe that we can already see three of the hooks that God could use to bring them down into that land:

1. Russia needs a warm-water entrance into the waterways of the world. Israel offers that, and Russia is moving in this direction. A few years ago I sat in the dining room on the top floor of the Hilton Hotel in Istanbul and watched Russian ships coming out of the Black Sea,

moving through the Bosporus, and heading for the Mediterranean Sea. This took place after the Six-Day War, and Russian naval strength had increased tremendously. What are the Russians looking for? They are looking for a warm-water port. Admiral Sergei Gorshkov made this statement, "The flag of the Soviet navy now proudly flies over the oceans of the world. Sooner or later the United States will have to understand that it no longer has mastery of the seas." Russia is looking for a warm-water port. Where are they going? All I know is that they are headed for the Mediterranean Sea. What nation along the east side of the Mediterranean would be suitable as a port? Israel certainly would be. Russia is interested in moving southward today. God has put a hook in their jaw.

2. God has a second hook—oil. The oil deposits of the Near East are essential for the survival of modern nations. Russia needs oil. To-day we are being constantly reminded that the world is running short of energy. Oil is one of the resources in short supply. As a result the world is turning to the places where they can get oil. There is oil in the Near East. Whether or not the oil is actually in the land of Israel is not the important thing. The important consideration is that, in spite of the strained relations between the Arabs and the Jews, a great deal of that oil is going through the land of Israel. When ships were not able to go through the Suez Canal, they put the oil off at a port which had been taken by Israel, and then the oil was taken across the land of Israel to the Mediterranean ports. As far back as 1955 I delivered a message stating that Russia was hungering for the Arabian oil. An editor of a paper in downtown Los Angeles heard my message and disagreed with it. Sometime later he made a trip over to the Near East area. When he returned, he wrote an article (and I have a copy of it) in which he said, "Russia hungers for Arabian oil." He changed his viewpoint after he had been to the Near East and had seen things with his own eyes. It is a pretty good hook God has in Russia's jaws because any modern nation must have oil.

3. The third hook concerns the Dead Sea. The mineral deposits in the Dead Sea are so great that they cannot be evaluated on today's mar-ket. Chemicals saturated in the water represent untold wealth. It is esti-mated that the Dead Sea contains two billion tons of potassium

chloride, which is potash—needed to sweeten and enrich the soil that is readily being depleted around the world, including our own area. The Dead Sea also contains twenty-two billion tons of magnesium chloride, twelve billion tons of sodium chloride, and six billion tons of calcium chloride. The Dead Sea, in addition to all of this, contains cerium, cobalt, manganese, and even gold. Believe me, friend, there is much effort being made today to extract this wealth from the Dead Sea.

If you had been around a few million years ago and had seen the Lord forming this earth, particularly the Dead Sea, you would probably have asked Him, "Why are you damming up that sea? You are going to have a pretty salty place." He would have replied, "I am baiting a hook." Then you would have said, "Baiting a hook for what?" Then the Lord would have said, "In a few million years there will be a nation in the north that I am going to bring into the land of Israel. I am just baiting one of the hooks of a little ahead of time." And that is what God has been doing—baiting a hook.

WHEN RUSSIA WILL INVADE ISRAEL

The question is: When will Russia come down? This is where many expositors disagree. There are those who believe that Russia will invade the land of Palestine at the end of this age, before the church is raptured. Others believe that Russia will come against Israel at the beginning of the Tribulation period, and others believe it will be at the end of the Tribulation. There are some who believe this will take place at the beginning of the Millennium. I am not going to discuss these different viewpoints in detail. My particular viewpoint is this: Russia will come in the "latter days" (v. 16); these "latter days" (as we have seen in the other prophets) is a technical term that specifically refers to the Tribulation period. These will be the days when the Antichrist comes to power, and he is going to come to power on a peace platform. As a result there will be a false peace for the first part of the Tribulation period; then in the midst of the seven years, Russia will come down from the north into the land of Israel. Russia will trigger the *Great* Tribulation by breaking the false peace made by the Antichrist and invading Israel.

> After many days thou shalt be visited: in the latter years
> thou shalt come into the land that is brought back from
> the sword, and is gathered out of many people, against
> the mountains of Israel, which have been always waste:
> but it is brought forth out of the nations, and they shall
> dwell safely all of them [Ezek. 38:8].

When Israel is back in the land, they will be under the domination of the Antichrist, who will make them believe that peace has come to the earth, that all of the problems of the earth are settled and they are entering the Millennium. But this is not true, and they will find in the midst of the Tribulation period that out of the north will come their enemy, Russia.

> And thou shalt come up against my people of Israel, as
> a cloud to cover the land; it shall be in the latter days,
> and I will bring thee against my land, that the heathen
> may know me, when I shall be sanctified in thee. O Gog,
> before their eyes [Ezek. 38:16].

Since Israel is dwelling in peace, and Antichrist has deceived everyone, God is Israel's only source of help. He Himself will deal with Russia. War will break out. The *Great* Tribulation will begin (which is the final three and one-half years of the Tribulation period) in all of its frenzied fury. The whole earth will be a holocaust. Judgments, one right after the other, will come upon the earth. War will reign. Christ said concerning this brief period, ". . . except those days should be shortened, there should no flesh be saved . . ." (Matt. 24:22).

I recommend that you read in your Bible the remainder of this chapter. This is God's judgment upon the invading armies of Russia.

RESULTS OF THE INVASION

Chapter 39 continues the prophecy against Gog and furnishes added details about the destruction of this formidable enemy.

And I will turn thee back, and leave but the sixth part of thee, and will cause thee to come up from the north parts, and will bring thee upon the mountains of Israel [Ezek. 39:2].

"Leave but the sixth part of thee" is literally "I will six thee," or better still, "I will afflict thee with six plagues." These plagues are listed in chapter 38 verse 22 as pestilence, blood, overflowing rain, great hailstones, fire, and brimstone. This is the way God destroyed Sodom and Gomorrah. According to the record, "Then the LORD rained upon Sodom and Gomorrah brimstone and fire from the LORD out of heaven" (Gen. 19:24). And this is exactly the way God intends to destroy this army which will come out of the north against His people to destroy them. You must remember that Russia has always been anti-Semitic. At the present writing the largest population of Jews— outside the land of Israel and the United States—is over there in Russia. We are hearing a great deal of criticism of Russia for not permitting the Jews to leave. Well, in these last days God will deal with Russia for its treatment of His people.

There is a message for us here. When God was ready to destroy Sodom and Gomorrah, Abraham thought He was being unjust. He asked God, "Will you destroy the righteous with the wicked? Will you spare the city if there are fifty righteous—forty-five—forty—thirty— twenty—ten?" God said no, He would not destroy the city if ten righteous were found there. But there were not ten, and God sent His angels to get Lot out of the city, saying that they could not destroy the city until Lot was out of it. My friend, this is one reason I believe that God will not let the Tribulation come until He takes His church—that is, all born-again believers—out of the world. Let me illustrate this with the following diagram:

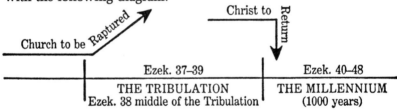

Church to be *Raptured*

Christi to **Return**

Ezek. 37–39   Ezek. 40–48

THE TRIBULATION   THE MILLENNIUM
Ezek. 38 middle of the Tribulation   (1000 years)

To put it very bluntly, all hell will break loose on the earth during the Tribulation period. It will be a frightful, terrible time. I don't understand the folk who insist that God's redeemed ones, which we designate as the church, will go through the Tribulation. The Bible makes it clear that those who will be witnessing on the earth during this time will be the 144,000 Jews.

God, having dealt in judgment with the enemy that invaded Israel from the north, allows Antichrist to be the world ruler for the remainder of the Tribulation period. Then the Lord Jesus Christ will come to the earth to establish His Kingdom; we have that pictured in chapter 19 of Revelation. In chapter 20 of the Book of Revelation the Kingdom, the Millennium, begins.

With these tremendous events in mind, it would be well to pause a moment and consider the material we have studied. After a careful examination of three of the four major prophets: Isaiah, Jeremiah, and Ezekiel, certain great principles emerge which the fourth prophet, Daniel, will confirm. These principles have an ageless application for nations of the world and for believers (when I say "believers," I am speaking about those who have trusted the Lord Jesus Christ as Savior and believe that the Bible is the Word of God). In Ezekiel we have seen God dealing with Israel. My friend, when God says "Israel" He means Israel; He does not mean the church. How some can believe that God means the church when He says Israel is a flip on the flying trapeze of theology that is beyond me. Let's allow God to mean what He says and realize that He has been dealing in these prophecies with the literal people of Israel. That is the correct interpretation. However, there is an application we can make since God's dealing with Israel is a microcosm of His dealings with the world in which we live. The principles God has used in dealing with His own people Israel are *eternal*, for they are linked to the character and attributes of God. I have stated some of them in the Books of Isaiah and Jeremiah, and now I am prepared to draw certain conclusions from Ezekiel.

No prophet emphasizes the glory and the holiness of God more then Ezekiel. He *saw* the glory of God—that was the great vision he had at the beginning of his book. He never forgot it. And we should not forget it either. His emphasis, therefore, is upon God's judgment.

God is longsuffering, not willing that any should perish, and He warned His people again and again that, if they did not turn to Him, He would judge Jerusalem. Then Jerusalem was destroyed, and Ezekiel offered the people encouragement as they looked into the future. "But," he said, "another enemy is coming." When the Lord Jesus Christ was on earth, He wept over the city of Jerusalem because He knew that Titus the Roman would be around in a few years to destroy the city, just as Nebuchadnezzar had done in the past.

Things were wrong in Jerusalem; and, if that city was to enjoy the blessings of God, those things had to be made right. The liars should cease lying; the thieves should cease stealing; the lawless should become law-abiding; and righteousness should prevail in the city. Only when God was acknowledged and respected in the land could blessing rest upon Jerusalem. Righteousness must prevail before any nation or individual can experience the love, mercy, and goodness of God. Jerusalem was *wrong*—the people were thinking wrong; they were acting wrong. They were in sin, and God was *right* in judging them. God never blesses that which is wrong.

This is made evident when we contrast Ezekiel with Jeremiah. I want you to notice this again because I consider it rather important. Jeremiah reveals the heart of God. God does not want to judge. As He said in Isaiah, judgment is *strange* work. He would rather save—that is His business. He is not willing that any should perish. He is very much involved with the human race. The great statement in John's Gospel is that He became *flesh* and came down here among us. This reveals His love and concern for us. It broke His heart that Jerusalem would be destroyed. Jesus wept over it just as Jeremiah had wept over it centuries before.

In Ezekiel we have something altogether different. At the very time Jerusalem was being destroyed, Ezekiel's wife died, and God forbad him to mourn or sorrow for her. He was to act like nothing happened. God wept over Jerusalem, but He did not mourn. He did not repent for what He had done, because He was right in doing it. God, with tears in His eyes, punished Jerusalem and destroyed the city, but He was doing that which was in keeping with His character. He did what was right because what God does is right. Paul asks, ". . . Is there unrighteousness with God? God forbid" (Rom 9:14). Of course there is no unrighteousness with God. Whatever God does is right. His glory is manifested in judgment. His grace is manifested in redemption. If God had not provided redemption for us, there would be no salvation for man whatsoever.

In chapters 38 and 39 of Ezekiel we saw that the kingdom in the north which is going to invade Israel (which I believe is Russia) will be destroyed in the future. The question is: Why will God destroy Russia? Let's read this verse again: "And thou shalt come up against my people of Israel, as a cloud to cover the land; it shall be in the latter days, and I will bring thee against my land, that the heathen may know me, when I shall be sanctified in thee, O Gog, before their eyes" (Ezek. 38:16). What is God going to do? He is going to destroy them. I can hear someone exclaim, "Do you mean God will actually do such a thing?" Certainly He will. The liberal theologian has a problem with the Creator destroying what He chooses, such as the Lord Jesus cursing a fig tree and also destroying a few pigs. I was in a conference one time when a man who was a liberal in his theology almost wept because Jesus destroyed those pigs (Matt. 8:30–32)! Yet every morning he ate bacon for breakfast! He was like the Walrus and the Carpenter who wept, but were busy eating oysters as fast as they could. I am not impressed with these people who get upset with God because He judges. I have a notion that God gets me a little upset with them.

Now let me cite two other verses:

And I will send a fire on Magog, and among them that dwell carelessly in the isles: and they shall know that I am the LORD.

So will I make my holy name known in the midst of my people Israel; and I will not let them pollute my holy name any more: and the heathen shall know that I am the LORD, the Holy One in Israel [Ezek. 39:6–7].

Is God going to destroy Russia? He says that He will send fire on Magog and among those that dwell securely in the coastlands. The question is: Where is God today? Why doesn't He move in defense of His people in our day? I shall never forget watching a newscast on television several years ago when a group of Christians appeared at the American Embassy in Moscow and appealed, actually weeping, for permission to leave Russia because of being persecuted. Our country did nothing. And the Russian soldiers came and took these people away. I waited for a long time to hear what had happened to them, but there was never a further word in the media. The Soviet authorities were never dealt with. And Russia has been guilty of more anti-Semitism than any other nation over a period of years. Oh, the injustice in the world! I see very little fear of God throughout the world. The feeling is that He is a jolly old Man who shuts His eyes to the injustice in the world. Why doesn't God move against injustice? Well, He *will* move when it is time. He will vindicate His glory, but He will not do it in a vindictive, revengeful, and petulant manner. He will judge, and when He does, there will be a respect and reverence for God in this world, and little man will bow before Him.

Romans 2:3 tells us, "And thinkest thou this, O man, that judgest them which do such things, and doest the same, that thou shalt escape the judgment of God?" Man is not going to escape judgment. He thinks he will get away with his sin, but he will not. In Hebrews 2:3 we read, "How shall we escape, if we neglect so great salvation; which at the first began to be spoken by the Lord, and was confirmed unto us by them that heard him." My friend, do you realize that this is a question which even God cannot answer? How *shall* we escape, if we neglect so great salvation? Well, we can't escape. There is no answer to that question.

Now let me use an old-fashioned expression that gags the liberal preachers (and also some evangelicals who are attempting to make the world a better place for people to go to hell in). Here it is: Hell, my friend, is an awful *reality*. You can interpret it any way you want to, but it is a place where a holy God puts those who are in rebellion against Him, those who sin with impunity, those who blaspheme God and His holy name at will, those who live like animals in the name of freedom but who are indulging in gross immorality. My friend, God's holy name is going to be vindicated.

How will God's holy name be vindicated? In love? He is demonstrating His love today in giving His Son. Those of us who name His name need to learn a lesson. We need to learn that we cannot trifle with Him. We cannot get familiar with Him. We cannot live as we please and then get buddy-buddy with Him. Our God is holy. Neither can we presume upon Him. We cannot sin and get by with it. If that were possible, then God would be no better than we are. Man is only a creature. The will of God will prevail, and our proper position is to bow before Him. Our only liberty today is in the will of God. He remembers that we are dust, but I can say with Paul, ". . . I obtained mercy . . ." (1 Tim. 1:13). My friend, if you deny Him, He will trample you under His feet. He has loved you enough to give His Son, but if you reject His mercy and grace, He will reject you. This is His universe, this is His earth, and He is running it according to His perfect plan. My friend, we need to get in step with Him.

CHAPTERS 40—48

THEME: Description of the millennial temple, worship in the millennial temple; return of the glory of the Lord

In this concluding section of the Book of Ezekiel we find a description of the millennial temple, the worship of the millennial temple, and a vision concerning the land.

THE MILLENNIAL TEMPLE

Chapters 40—42 contain a description of the millennial temple. Now since this is the millennial temple, I expect to see it and maybe go into it, but I don't intend to worship there. The temple will be here on this earth, but I am going to be in the place which is described in Revelation 21—the New Jerusalem. That will be the address of the believer for eternity. If you want to give someone your address as a believer for eternity, I don't know what street you will be on (I hope I'm on Glory Blvd.), but I do know the city—it will be the New Jerusalem. One thing that John tells us about this city is, "And I saw no temple therein: for the Lord God Almighty and the Lamb are the temple of it" (Rev. 21:22). Therefore the church is going to be in a place where there won't be a temple; we won't need one, but the earth will have one for the duration of the Millennium at least. I rather like the fact that we won't have a temple because, very candidly, I have never gone in much for ritual. I'm going to be delighted to be up there with the Lord God and the Lamb as the temple of the New Jerusalem. We will be with them, and I cannot even conceive how wonderful that is going to be.

We have seen a certain progress and development in the Book of Ezekiel: after the enemy is put down, Israel enters the Millennium, and there will be a temple here on this earth. We are talking about the earth, and that means we are talking about Israel and the gentile nations which will be saved. The church of Christ is up yonder with Him in the New Jerusalem at this time.

> **In the five and twentieth year of our captivity, in the beginning of the year, in the tenth day of the month, in the fourteenth year after that the city was smitten, in the selfsame day the hand of the LORD was upon me, and brought me thither [Ezek. 40:1].**

Jerusalem has been destroyed and the temple is burned, but Ezekiel is to be shown now the temple that will be in that city during the millennial Kingdom.

> **In the visions of God brought he me into the land of Israel, and set me upon a very high mountain, by which was as the frame of a city on the south.**
>
> **And he brought me thither, and, behold, there was a man, whose appearance was like the appearance of brass, with a line of flax in his hand, and a measuring reed; and he stood in the gate [Ezek. 40:2–3].**

Every time in Scripture that we find a man with a measuring rod—it generally is an angel, and it is an angel here—it means that God is getting ready to move again in dealing with His earthly people. We find this again in the minor prophets and in the Book of Revelation.

> **And the man said unto me, Son of man, behold with thine eyes, and hear with thine ears, and set thine heart upon all that I shall shew thee; for to the intent that I might shew them unto thee art thou brought hither: declare all that thou seest to the house of Israel [Ezek. 40:4].**

It is my personal feeling that Ezekiel was brought literally to Jerusalem and shown there a vision of the millennial temple of the future.

> And behold a wall on the outside of the house round
> about, and in the man's hand a measuring reed of six
> cubits long by the cubit and an hand breadth: so he mea-
> sured the breadth of the building, one reed; and the
> height, one reed [Ezek. 40:5].

Beginning with verse 5 and continuing through these chapters we are
given a great deal of detailed information concerning the temple
which I will not go into. Its environs are given to us, and it will obviously be a thing of great beauty.

> And in the porch of the gate were two tables on this side,
> and two tables on that side, to slay thereon the burnt
> offering and the sin offering and the trespass offering
> [Ezek. 40:39].

In verses 39–42 we find that the Mosaic system will be restored with
the reinstating of the levitical liturgy and the burnt offering, the sin
offering, and the trespass offering.

> Four tables were on this side, and four tables on that
> side, by the side of the gate; eight tables, whereupon
> they slew their sacrifices [Ezek. 40:41].

There will be sacrifices offered in the millennial temple. I will discuss
this further in chapter 45.

> And without the inner gate were the chambers of the
> singers in the inner court, which was at the side of the
> north gate; and their prospect was toward the south:
> one at the side of the east gate having the prospect
> toward the north [Ezek. 40:44].

There will also be music and singers in the temple.

So he measured the court, an hundred cubits long, and an hundred cubits broad, foursquare; and the altar that was before the house [Ezek. 40:47].

Our attention is again called to the fact that there will be an altar for sacrifices. In the Holy Land Hotel in Jerusalem there is a miniature replica of the city as it was in the days of Herod and the Lord Jesus. Actually it is quite a large model, and as far as I could tell when examining it closely, there is no altar for sacrifice in the temple model—it has been left out. The orthodox Jews are a little embarrassed by an altar, and the liberal Jews want to get rid of it altogether. However, in the millennial temple there will be an altar.

WORSHIP IN THE MILLENNIAL TEMPLE

Chapters 43—46 describe the worship of the millennial temple. As we consider the millennial temple, we need to remember that in the last days of the temple of Solomon, the *Shekinah* glory, the presence of God, was absent. However, here in chapter 43 the glory returns to the temple, and, as we see the worship in the millennial temple, the One Israel worships is now in the temple. He is none other than the Lord Jesus Christ.

Afterward he brought me to the gate, even the gate that looketh toward the east:

And, behold, the glory of the God of Israel came from the way of the east: and his voice was like a noise of many waters: and the earth shined with his glory [Ezek. 43:1–2].

The glory of God comes from the east and fills the temple. This is the return of Christ to the earth, and He brings the *Shekinah* glory with Him. When he came to Bethlehem more than nineteen hundred years ago, the glory was not with Him.

> And the glory of the LORD came into the house by the way
> of the gate whose prospect is toward the east [Ezek.
> 43:4].

Apparently the Lord will come from the east. We will look at this again in chapter 44.

> And thou shalt give to the priests the Levites that be of
> the seed of Zadok, which approach unto me, to minister
> unto me, saith the Lord GOD, a young bullock for a sin
> offering [Ezek. 43:19].

In this section we are dealing with the worship in the temple. The sacrifices offered will be memorial in character. They will look back to the work of Christ on the Cross, as the offering of the Old Testament anticipated His sacrifice. In chapter 45 we will go into more detail about this.

In chapter 44 Ezekiel is told that a prince will enter the city through the eastern gate:

> Then he brought me back the way of the gate of the out-
> ward sanctuary which looketh toward the east; and it
> was shut.

> Then said the LORD unto me; This gate shall be shut, it
> shall not be opened, and no man shall enter in by it;
> because the LORD, the God of Israel, hath entered in by
> it, therefore it shall be shut.

> It is for the prince; the prince, he shall sit in it to eat
> bread before the LORD; he shall enter by the way of the
> porch of that gate, and shall go out by the way of the
> same [Ezek. 44:1-3].

The eastern gate of present-day Jerusalem is shut—it is completely walled up. Some of my premillennial brethren feel that this is a fulfillment of these verses in Ezekiel and that the gate will not be opened again until the Messiah comes. I have two objections to this viewpoint that I would like to mention.

My first point is that the prince mentioned here who is coming is *not* the Lord Jesus Christ. Ezekiel tells us that this prince offers a sacrifice and worships God (chs. 45–46); therefore he cannot be the Lord Jesus. The Lord Jesus *is* God, and He never has and never will offer a sacrifice. It is not necessary for Him to do so, for He is still able to say, "Which of you convinceth [convicteth] me of sin? . . ." (John 8:46). This prince is not the Lord Jesus Christ. I personally feel that the prince is David. There are many fine men who do not agree that it is David, but they do agree that it is not the Lord Jesus. Many of them feel that the prince is simply another man in the line of David.

My second objection is that the gate in question is obviously not the gate of the city—it is the gate of the temple. It is true that the temple is not there yet, and the temple must be built before any of this can take place. The walled-up gate to the city has nothing to do with it. He probably will come through that eastern gate of the city, but it could be the present gate, or the wall could be torn down and an entirely new wall and gate be built before then. We must remember that the wall that is there now is neither the wall that Christ knew nor that Ezekiel knew—both of those walls have long since been destroyed.

Chapter 45 tells us that the Feast of the Passover will be kept:

Thus saith the Lord God; In the first month, in the first day of the month, thou shalt take a young bullock without blemish, and cleanse the sanctuary:

And the priest shall take of the blood of the sin offering, and put it upon the posts of the house, and upon the four corners of the settle of the altar, and upon the posts of the gate of the inner court.

And so thou shalt do the seventh day of the month for every one that erreth, and for him that is simple: so shall ye reconcile the house.

> In the first month, in the fourteenth day of the month, ye
> shall have the passover, a feast of seven days; unleav-
> ened bread shall be eaten.
>
> And upon that day shall the prince prepare for himself
> and for all the people of the land a bullock for a sin of-
> fering [Ezek. 45:18-22].

The Passover definitely refers to Christ: we are told in 1 Corinthians 5:7, ". . . For even Christ our passover is sacrificed for us."

At this point we must answer a major question: Since all the sacrifices of the Old Testament were fulfilled in Christ, why are they restored again during the Millennium? This is a major argument that amillennialists have against the premillennial position. I personally find no conflict here. I feel that the sacrifices offered during the Millennium are going to look back to the coming of Christ and His death upon the Cross in the same way that in our day the Lord's Supper looks back to them. Someone will ask why the *literal* offering of sacrifices will be necessary. My friend, the human family has a great deal of difficulty learning a lesson. For the same reason, I believe that the literal blood of Christ is going to be in heaven. It will be there to reveal to us the horrible pit out of which we were digged. Our salvation from sin and hell unto heaven was a pretty big job, one that only God could undertake. The blood of Christ will be in heaven to remind the church of this, and the sacrifices will also be restored here on earth to reveal to the people of Israel how they were redeemed.

A VISION CONCERNING THE LAND

In chapters 47—48 Ezekiel is given a picture of the land during the millennial Kingdom.

> Afterward he brought me again unto the door of the
> house; and, behold, waters issued out from under the
> threshold of the house eastward: for the forefront of
> the house stood toward the east, and the waters came

down from under from the right side of the house, at the
south side of the altar.

Then brought he me out of the way of the gate northward, and led me about the way without unto the utter
gate by the way that looketh eastward; and, behold,
there ran out waters on the right side [Ezek. 47:1-2].

"Behold, waters issued out from under the threshold of the house
eastward"—that is, they came from the altar. That is where all blessings originate—at the altar. Everything that comes to us by way of
blessings comes through the death of Christ for you and me upon the
cross.

The water here is a type of the Holy Spirit, and many spiritual les-
sons may be drawn from this passage:

And when the man that had the line in his hand went
forth eastward, he measured a thousand cubits, and he
brought me through the waters; the waters were to the
ankles [Ezek. 47:3].

"The waters were to the ankles." This speaks of the walk of the believer in the Spirit.

Again he measured a thousand, and brought me
through the waters; the waters were to the knees. Again
he measured a thousand, and brought me through; the
waters were to the loins [Ezek. 47:4].

"The waters were to the knees"—this speaks of prayer.
"The waters were to the loins." We are to gird up our loins for service. The walk and service of a believer rest upon the redemption we
have in Christ.

Afterward he measured a thousand; and it was a river
that I could not pass over: for the waters were risen, wa-

**ters to swim in, a river that could not be passed over
[Ezek. 47:5].**

"Waters to swim in" indicates the fullness of the Spirit. This looks
forward to the day when God will pour out His Spirit upon these people; He is not doing that today.

**Now when I had returned, behold, at the bank of the
river were very many trees on the one side and on the
other [Ezek. 47:7].**

"Many trees"—this is the fruit that will be in our lives.

I have given you an *application* of this passage which we can make
to our own lives. However, its *interpretation* for the people of Israel is
that there will be an eternal spring of water coming out of that altar in
that day which will bring blessing to that land. And, my friend, they
need water in that land today.

Chapter 48 gives us the division of the land among the twelve
tribes. Of particular interest to us is the tribe of Dan:

**Now these are the names of the tribes. From the north
end to the coast of the way of Hethlon, as one goeth to
Hamath, Hazarenan, the border of Damascus northward, to the coast of Hamath; for these are his sides east
and west; a portion for Dan.**

**And by the border of Dan, from the east side unto the
west side, a portion for Asher [Ezek. 48:1–2].**

The tribe of Dan is present in the Millennium although it is absent
from those sealed in the Great Tribulation period (see Rev. 7:4–8).
Danites do not serve in the Great Tribulation, but the grace of God
brings them into the Millennium. We, too, are saved by grace but re-
warded for service.

The Book of Ezekiel has closed with a picture of the city, the millennial temple, and the land during the Millennium—all the curse is removed. What a picture we have here!

It was round about eighteen thousand measures: and the name of the city from that day shall be, The LORD is there [Ezek. 48:35].

The prophet Ezekiel closes on a high note: "The LORD is there."

BIBLIOGRAPHY
(Recommended for Further Study)

Alexander, Ralph. *Ezekiel*. Chicago, Illinois: Moody Press, 1976. (Fine, inexpensive survey.)

Feinberg, Charles L. *The Prophecy of Ezekiel*. Chicago, Illinois: Moody Press, 1969. (Excellent.)

Gaebelein, Arno C. *The Prophet Ezekiel*. 1918. Reprint. Neptune, New Jersey: Loizeaux Brothers, 1972. (Excellent.)

Grant, F. W. *The Numerical Bible, Ezekiel*. 6 vols. Neptune, New Jersey: Loizeaux Brothers, n.d.

Gray, James M. *Synthetic Bible Studies*. Old Tappan, New Jersey: Fleming H. Revell, Co., 1906.

Ironside, H. A. *Expository Notes on Ezekiel*. Neptune, New Jersey: Loizeaux Brothers, 1959.

Jensen, Irving L. *Ezekiel and Daniel*. Chicago, Illinois: Moody Press. (Self study guide.)

Kelly, William. *Notes on Ezekiel*. 1876. Reprint. Addison, Illinois: Bible Truth Publishers.

Sauer, Erich. *The Dawn of World Redemption*. Grand Rapids, Michigan: William B. Eerdmans Publishing Co., 1951. (An excellent Old Testament survey.)

Scroggie, W. Graham. *The Unfolding Drama of Redemption*. Grand Rapids, Michigan, Zondervan Publishing House, 1970. (An excellent survey and outline of the Old Testament.)

Unger, Merrill F. *Unger's Bible Handbook*. Chicago, Illinois: Moody Press, 1966.

Unger, Merrill F. *Unger's Commentary on the Old Testament*, Vol. 2. Chicago, Illinois: Moody Press, 1982. (Highly recommended.)